Against the Storm
A Harvey Story

Greg Etzel

ISBN: 0-9745923-5-8

For my family….

I. Staring into the Sun

There are 6.5 million stories about Hurricane Harvey. This is mine.

Oddly enough, it begins in Loup City, Nebraska, far from the threatening skies over the Gulf of Mexico. It was the Monday of the week of the storm, before I had lost track of what day it was. I was on vacation. I had taken the week off from work to move my oldest son, Zachary, back to his dorm for his second year of college. He studies, usually more than his demanding father gives him credit for, at Rhodes College in Memphis, and I enjoyed the prior weekend getting him settled back into his now familiar academic environs. I was rather envious, to be honest, wishing I were in his youthful shoes.

It would resonate more deeply with me later that my envy of his position was entirely reliant on the fact I had made it to where I was at this point in my life, which I considered to be a generally good place. I had a feeling of satisfaction that comes from "knowing how the story turns out" and ignores the vast uncertainty that must exist in the mind of a boy, now a man, one year and many miles removed from his childhood home. The fortuitous unfolding of the intervening 30 years of *my* life gave me a much different, and fonder, perspective of his stage in life than I was willing, or capable, to recall. The anxiety of the unknown was absent from my envy.

Zach was preparing himself in college for a

world of unprecedented technological and economic change, littered with opportunities and risks, not all within his ability to control. His situation, without my knowing at the time, served as the perfect preface to the coming storm. In a week, I would find myself peering from the second story window of my home, watching the rain, and grappling with the nervous uncertainty that goes hand in hand with the benefits of youth.

But as I left Zach in Memphis to make my way toward Nebraska on the Sunday before the storm, I longed to be a college student again. It was perhaps in the spirit of this yearning that Zach's move in was only the first leg in a road trip that brought me to the starting point of this story. I was meeting my mother, several aunts and uncles, cousins, second cousins, and cousins by varying degrees of removal for the finale of a large family reunion weekend in Cedar Rapids, Nebraska. The reunion weekend corresponded, by virtue of the precision planning of my Uncle Glenn, with the first solar eclipse over the continental United States in 100 years. My uncle works for NASA at the Johnson Space Center in Houston. Cedar Rapids, Nebraska, is the ancestral home of my maternal grandmother, and remains the home of many of her (and my, though more distant) relatives; and Nebraska was one of the states through which the shadow of the sun would pass in totality on Monday, August 21, 2017. To my uncle, this situation absolutely screamed for a family reunion weekend on August 19 and 20, followed by an eclipse watch party on the

21st.

   When I arrived at the house of my mother's cousins, Bill and Rita, I had either not met these *distant Nebraska relatives* or had not seen them since I was a child. We were connected by the thinnest strand of familial bond, stretched across generations of time and miles of geographic space. Yet, I was welcomed into their home, and the home of more cousins, Steve and Peg, where I would stay the night, as if I were a direct member of their families. In the comfort of their hospitality, I visited with familiar and unfamiliar relatives alike. I learned in my conversations that the crop interrupting the miles and miles of rolling cornfields on Highway 34 (as well as the other highways throughout Eastern Nebraska) is soybean. In fact, I learned more about agricultural sciences in one evening than I had in my entire life. My distant admiration for farmers was transformed into an immediate fascination.

   They explained to me how, from before the seed is planted through to harvest, every step is precisely measured and controlled. The hybrid of seed, the spacing of crop rows, the timing of nutrients farmers add to the soil, whether and what type of pest control, the patterns for harvest— *every* single detail—designed to maximize the yield value per acre. Far from the Luddite stereotype mythically portrayed in contrasting *urban industrialization* and *rural agriculture,* they embraced technology more readily than most urbanites. Advanced software, automated drones, chemistry, and genetics were as much a part of their everyday lives as the physical toil that comes with farming. And yet with all of this technology and planning, each of these multi-generational family farmers would readily admit to knowing one element in the process they can't control—the rain.

"The rain comes when it comes."

That's what they told me. You can design your crop rows, perfect your seed hybrid, and develop your nutrient plan, but if the rain doesn't come, it won't matter. "The rain comes when it comes." It's funny how little phrases like that stick out when you find yourself watching the waters rise. At the time, it seemed like just a part of polite conversation, a farmer's proverb, to take with a heavy grain of my urban salt. Like 6.5 million others in the Houston area, and even more throughout southeast Texas, I would soon experience the truth in their simple wisdom.

It's no coincidence the church is the central building in all of the farm towns I drove into throughout the rolling corn- (and soybean-) covered hills of Nebraska. Farmers know what they cannot control better than anyone else. Faith is their deliverer. You go through the labor and the toil of developing seed hybrids, designing rows, and establishing nutrient balances, because you *believe* the rains will come. But that's always the best you have. Farming and faith are natural companions. It all made more sense to me in hindsight. In a sheltered, air-conditioned suburban home, with a grocery store around the corner, I was several steps removed from the harvest cycle, and perhaps took it all for granted. However, as I slept at Steve and Peg's on Sunday night, these conversations and observations were settling themselves deep in my restful mind.

Monday, August 21, 2017, started as a beautiful sunny morning in Loup City, Nebraska. Loup City is about a 45-minute drive from Cedar Rapids and, while it somewhat frivolously uses the term *city* to describe itself, it was nevertheless a lovely place from which to observe the eclipse. We drove to Steve's farmhouse on the outskirts of this city of 900 people in another area surrounded by rolling hills of corn. Loup City was selected by my uncles, Glenn and Wayne, both engineers, as the location for our eclipse watch party because it lay almost exactly on the center line of the totality path. This would ensure the maximum amount of time, still barely more than two minutes, during which we could look upon the eclipsed-sun with our naked eyes. I had driven nearly 1,000 miles, across six states, to stare at the sun for two minutes. I told you it was a college-kid-brained idea. But I had the vacation time to use, so I followed my boyish impulses.

I was happy I did. Whereas on Sunday evening, the family who had remained in Cedar Rapids for generations gave an education on agricultural sciences to the urbanites from Texas, Monday morning shifted to lessons from the generation whose parents followed NASA from the farmlands. My grandfather, whose service in the army air corps found him engaged in the development of pressurized suits for high altitude flights, moved to Houston to take a shot on an upstart government organization that would end up planting a United States flag on the surface of the moon within a decade after his arrival. He didn't have a college degree, but was one of the sharpest engineers NASA had working on the development of the iconic astronaut suit every kid dreams of wearing. His sons, drawn themselves into the science of flight and space, and formally educated in them at Texas A&M, gave an impromptu lecture on the unfolding solar event much to the rapt attention of the Nebraskan relatives and other farm hands who had gathered in interest, if not of the eclipse, then at least of the crowd gathered in the farmhouse yard in the middle of a work day eating hamburgers and freshly made applesauce.

Presented as they were to me in back-to-back family meals, it was easy to see the connection between the worlds of those who *stayed on the farm* and those who *went to the city*. Both were fully immersed in their trades, keen observers of nature and its laws. The similarity in their core values translated in different ways in the diverse occupations to which they had dedicated themselves, but I could see a clear unity in principle. I attributed this to the common familial heritage – a heritage I shared, one generation further removed.

I confess I found a comforting certitude in the *NASA generation's* lecture. Wayne and Glenn described how the solar event was capable of being calculated such that one could predict to the exact second the time the eclipse would occur where we were in Loup City. I marveled at the thought that giant balls of gas and mounds of rock hurtling through space at thousands of miles an hour, and separated by vast emptiness and unseen matter, were somehow capable of being measured such that engineers could know with certitude at 11:33:18 AM on Monday, August 21, 2017, in Loup City, Nebraska, the moon would begin traversing the sun. I thought of it as a testimony to human progress, to the triumph of intellect, and it provided a degree of security in knowing there was a predictability to our universe so unfathomably huge.

But the farmers' wit raised the specter of a deeper truth, "Now, if you could give me *that* kind of predictability on the rain, we'd be on to something," Bill said with a wry smile. We all had a loud chuckle. Even the engineers would concede that *predicting* and *controlling* are two entirely distinct concepts. The engineers had limits to their scientific certitude. The rain comes when it comes. You can predict when the eclipse is going to happen, but you can't prevent it from happening. You can tell a farmer *when* it's going to rain, but you can't *make* it rain. Nor, as it would turn out, can you make it stop.

Nevertheless, the predictability of my professorial uncles was spot on. From 11:38:18 AM until 12:57:16 PM, we watched (with NASA-approved eclipse glasses) the moon crawl steadily, at a barely perceptible speed, across the face of the sun. Yet, as Wayne had explained, the moon was actually hurtling by at nearly 2,300 miles per hour. Our perceptions are merely relative to our own speed and place on the planet. It was all quite a lot to take in.

Observing the solar eclipse and enjoying the connections between family across distant generations and walks of life, I helped myself to a third serving of applesauce and made sure I had cued up some appropriate background music. I find the right music can enhance any event, and certainly the eclipse offered the opportunity to dust off some classics. Obviously, Bonnie Tyler's *Total Eclipse of the Heart* was front and center on the place list, which culminated with Pink Floyd's *Eclipse*. I imagined it was a pretty standard set for such an event, really.

Using an open black umbrella as the moon and my bright yellow shirt as the sun, my Aunt Joan and mother helped me send an *eclipse re-enactment* (or *pre-enactment* as the case may be) video to my children who were stuck in school watching a partial eclipse in Houston. My Uncle Paul and cousin Brian set up a camera with a large telephoto lens, complete with special filters, and were frequently ensuring that the positioning and settings were just right for the big shot to come. I felt a sense of alignment, not unlike the one underway above me in the skies. Perhaps, I was just searching for deeper meanings in the eclipse to justify my long drive, or perhaps it was another simple observation in passing made starker by the experience of the storm to come.

As the moment of totality approached, we felt a cool calm air settle in around us, while the gentle gloaming gave way to an early evening-like darkness. Donkeys were braying, birds had returned to their nests, and the poor dog didn't know what the hell was going on. Yet, an eerie tranquility surrounded us as the bright *diamond ring* flash from the sun announced the start of totality.

"You can take off the glasses now," Glenn advised us we were safe to stare directly at the now fully shadowed sun. "We have two minutes and now 15 seconds."

Two minutes. That's it. What was I going to do? We had talked during the morning about the many anomalies of light potentially observable — apparently it is possible to see the wave patterns of the wind in whatever breeze was perceptible during the eclipse. Stars and planets not normally observable in the daylight were capable of being seen in the darkness of the total eclipse. Indeed, everything that is observable was cast in this unique and amazing light. But only for two minutes and 18 seconds, and I had already wasted at least ten seconds just thinking about it.

I gazed directly at the eclipsed sun. I then brought my eyes down through the field of daytime stars and into the pinkish-purple and orange hue glowing along the horizon line in all directions. I'd never seen such a color before. Its beauty is beyond my capacity to describe. I thought it poignant that even in the darkest shadow of the sun, a soft light glows on the horizon. It was not truly dark even when the sun is totally blocked.

Unsure of how much time I had spent gazing at the 360-degree horizon, I decided to pass on other potential observations and cast my gaze back toward the sun. It was remarkable. I felt a kindred spirit with the earliest of humans whom I imagined must have been frightened to their core—the great sun, giver of life and light, held back by the darkness in the middle of the day. How profoundly must they have felt (and likely feared) at the moment they observed an eclipse for the first time. Everything in their world they had taken for granted was called into question—the sun itself was just blotted out!

I found my focus being urged by the mesmerizing waves of the sun's corona into the center of the shadow—to the darkest point in the deep blue-toned blackness of the moon's shadow. This rare cosmic alignment presented me the opportunity to cast my eyes upon the object that would otherwise blind me. Into the shadow I longingly cast my gaze. I recalled my Nietzsche from professor Solomon's philosophy class in college, and his oft quoted phrase, "When you stare into the abyss, the abyss also stares at you."

I felt like that's exactly what I was doing. The

glow of the sun's ultra-white crown danced around the darkness of the shadowy abyss, as if marking a hidden treasure. It reminded me of the old video games I used to play with the kids that would have certain important items glow around the edges so they were highlighted for the player to find. I was similarly being pulled into whatever lay at the center of the eclipse. Thusly, I spent whatever time I had left transfixed on the golden-ringed shadow.

Whatever time I had left was not much, as a great flash announced the sun's slow return to its unfettered dominance over the sky. Even the slightest sliver of its light was too blinding to observe with the naked eye, and so the NASA-approved glasses went back on. The darkness was over. Two minutes and 18 seconds. That was it. About half a TV commercial break. And yet it was somehow long enough to be worth every mile I had traveled. This brief glimpse into totality was an invitation to a deeper question: What did I see? And what did the abyss see when it stared back at me?

Once we had all had a moment to take the event in, we gathered around and compared our observations, at least on the physical level. My Uncle Paul's camera captured a great shot of the total eclipse. We passed his camera around as if to have an instantaneous reminder of what we had literally just witnessed. We celebrated the passing of totality with some Mississippi Mudslides, recommended by Bill as the drink most befitting the occasion. I certainly wouldn't argue with him, as they were a delicious compliment to the entire eclipse feast. With a toast, it was over. The party wrapped up, and the farmers got right back to their work day. We Houstonians prepared for the long two-day drives ahead.

Before we departed, our Nebraska family loaded us up with a giant bag of fresh corn straight from their fields, which found its way into the back of my car. They passed along some fertilizer combinations for my mother and aunt, who were going to try use some of the agricultural knowledge they had acquired in their home gardens. Well, except maybe for the use of drones. Steve also gave us some of the honey he uses to make his applesauce, which I could not get enough of. The honey made it into my uncles' van, a wise maneuver on their part. As Glenn remarked, "I think they'd have given us the shirt off their backs, if we didn't stop them."

Their kindness, and their corn, accompanied me as I began to make my long drive back home. I queued up Paul Simon and started the journey with *Homeward Bound.* Its melancholy tune seemed to match my mood. I longed to be with Dedra and the kids, who had already started school and were unable to make the epic road trip. (They were not overly disappointed by missing the experience, after enduring a 10-day road trip last summer). Embarking with hugs from Nebraska, I made my way over two days to Hondo, Texas, where I had been instructed by Dedra to meet my father-in-law in order to pick up a quarter of a cow we had apparently purchased. I was hoping it was already butchered.

Now, there is a lot of time to think between Nebraska and Texas, and with apologies to my Kansan and Oklahoman friends, there ain't a whole heck of a lot to look at. The astronomy lessons of the day were at the front of my mind, and I began thinking of my drive in cosmic terms. I was traveling 1,000 miles. It would take me two days. It was 9.2 million miles from the earth to the sun. At my driving pace, it would take me 18,400 days to drive that distance—50 years. If I would have been put in a car traveling to the sun at my birth, I would still not be there. Although, I recognized uncomfortably, I would be alarmingly close—how did I get this old already?

My mind continued making rudimentary calculations. Moreover, the sun was just the *closest* star in a universe billions of light-years wide and long. Thinking of myself in the context of the vastness of distance and time on this astronomical scale gave me a cold, empty feeling. Measuring oneself against the infinite will have that effect, I suppose. Maybe this is what it means to look into the abyss? I recalled my thoughts as I was staring into the darkness of the *totality.* The question lingered—what did the *abyss* see? It seemed the invitation to introspection could not be withdrawn or revoked.

Fortunately, I shifted my thoughts with the changing borders. Texas brought me the comfortable feel of home, even though I still had 500 miles to drive. Crossing the Red River brought my thoughts from the cold reaches of the distant stars to the warmth of more familiar environs. This long road trip was nearing its finale. Little did I know it was really only the beginning of my journey. That's how life is, I suppose.

As I pulled into Hondo on Tuesday night, I didn't even know a tropical storm was brewing in the Gulf of Mexico. In fact, as I arrived, it occurred to me, with a great degree of wonder, that I had been driving for five straight days, for over 2,000 miles, across now eight states, and I had not even encountered the slightest rain shower. This was quite remarkable. In fact, I'm not sure I had ever experienced such a smooth drive. But my Harvey story has to begin in Nebraska, where the long roots of family and the simple wisdom of farmers would serve as illumination when the skies would darken in the days ahead. Yes, my Harvey story began when I stared into the sun.

The rain comes when it comes.

II. The Challenge

      My father-in-law greeted me with a warm smile. And a quarter of a cow, butchered as hoped, packed in an ice chest, and ready to go. Chuck wore his smile naturally; whether by his own inborn personality trait or as the byproduct of a life's service as a Lutheran pastor, it may be difficult for even him to know. He saved me another few hours of driving to the town where "our cow" was butchered with his own errand earlier that afternoon. After five days of driving, I was grateful to trim any remaining fat, if I may be forgiven the pun, from my schedule before finally getting home. His thoughtfulness came as naturally to him as his smile and suffered from the same conundrum of origin.

      His daughter bore the same traits, whether by nature or example; ones that drew me to her 28 years earlier. She had given me specific instructions to ensure that the meat from our cow remained frozen solid, which meant she did not want the meat sitting in an ice chest for long periods of time for fear of potential bacterial growth. She was exceedingly risk averse in matters of biological pathogens; and I found no reasonable counterpoints to her concerns that would justify any objection to her request. I relayed my instructions to Chuck.

      "Oh, you don't need to worry about that. I've packed it down with eight pounds of dry ice. That stuff will stay frozen in there for a week," he responded with a plan that, while inconsistent with the letter of my instructions seemed to provide the necessary overkill Dedra would appreciate.

"Well, sounds like that will work to me. I only need half a day to get it to our freezer at home." I acknowledged the fact that I was in agreement with the new plan. "That should keep it solid and safe. I suppose it's extra sensitive to bacteria being antibiotic free and all?" I joked.

We packed the ice chest into the back of my SUV, where it would spend the night with another ice chest filled with chilled Nebraska corn. Glancing at them side by side, it occurred to me that perhaps we were taking the farm-to-table trend to some unnecessary extremes. With the wagon loaded, we walked back inside, poured ourselves a glass of wine, and sat down to the already-on TV. It was tuned to the Weather Channel.

This, in and of itself, would be nothing out of the ordinary. Chuck grew up on a farm; his parents were farmers not unlike those of my mother's relatives. A different calling from the one that lured my grandfather from the farm to the city urged Chuck into the seminary and a life as an ordained Lutheran pastor. For most of his adult life, he made his family's home in New Braunfels, Texas, where he preached for many years, and kept an abundant home garden as a vestige of his deep farming roots. With such an upbringing, weather was always of interest to him.

It occurred to me, albeit later, that, like a

farmer, a pastor too has a heightened sense of what lies beyond human control. They observe both the joys and the tragedies of the parishioners in their church community. For every wedding or baptism, there are funerals and families grappling with an unexpected crises or disease. When these unforeseen events unfold in people's lives, the pastor offers words of faith as a deliverer from the calamities beyond their control. The weather is a reminder of the power we do not possess, and farmer and pastor alike know it well. You can only *watch* the weather. There is nothing you can do to *change* it.

"They say it may re-form and come up into Corpus," he said. Corpus, or Corpus Christi by its formal name, was right in the middle of the long Texas coastline, and as a lifelong Houstonian my ears perked up. These tropical systems can go anywhere the strong upper level air currents and pockets of air pressure take them. But it always seemed to me like they turn north and northeast as they approach the coast, making Houston, which lies northeast of Corpus Christi, a potential impact zone. So, I would say I was at least introduced to Harvey on Tuesday night.

He didn't really look like much at first. They never do—at first. It was *just* a tropical storm when it wandered over the Yucatan Peninsula earlier in the week and found itself little more than a weakened mass of clouds struggling to re-form as it emerged in the Gulf of Mexico. I'm not even sure it bore a name at that point. Just a generic storm. But the Gulf of Mexico is very warm in August, and all of the elements for Harvey's rise were in place. I watched the TV with half interest as we conversed. Hondo stood to get some much-needed rain, after a hot, dry summer. Chuck's brother, Leroy, and his wife, Linda, lived in Corpus Christi, but the storm hadn't yet rated much more than *keep an eye on* status at this point.

We shifted our conversation to catching up on family members and then turned in for the night. I slept the slumber of a man knowing it was his last night sleeping in another person's bed. I was up with the sun on Wednesday with a late morning/noon arrival time projected in Houston. My farm-to-table supplies were still ice cold and set for transport. I was ready to finish my journey.

Driving due east early in the morning from Hondo to Houston on the combination of Highway 90 and Interstate 10 that connects the cities, I was taunted by the sun. It dared me to look upon it in its full, un-shadowed glory. *"Haha! Look at me now eclipse chaser! Look at me!"* It seemed to beckon to me. Every shiny surface flashed a jarring glare, piercing my focus with blades of white light. With my sunglasses on, window shade tilted just right, and eyes down on the road in front of me I made my way along the highway cautiously enduring its stern rebuke.

The drive through the expanding metropolitan areas of San Antonio was cast in this bright glowing early-morning light. San Antonio was a favorite vacation destination for my parents when I was growing up as a kid. I fondly remembered the many childhood trips, and those memories contrasted with the much bigger city before me now. Sprawling like every major Texas city into its vast rural surroundings, the San Antonio I visited as a boy was surrounded by miles upon miles of urban and suburban neighborhoods. Hondo seemed even closer to the city than it did just the year before.

I have driven the I-10 corridor between San Antonio (or Columbus) and Houston more times than I would like to count. It was *always* the worst part of any returning road trip for me. Familiar paths seem the longest to tread. My audio book complete, and not in the mood for music, I tried to catch some sports radio and see what was going on with the Astros, who were having a historic baseball season. I was getting close enough to the city to pick up some AM stations. But then again, I wasn't. Downtown, Houston's center, was 50 miles away.

When I think back to my memories of a lifetime of drives, it's this portion of Interstate 10, or I-10 as locals call it, that stands out as having changed the most. I remember my father stopping in Katy, west of Houston, for gas or snacks as the first little town we came upon once we were outside Houston. That *little* town is now a major city in its own right, with several massive high schools (and the Texas-sized football stadiums that goes with them), large specialty medical centers, retail shops, and dining establishments, and the dividing line

between it and Houston is indistinguishable. The
four- or six-lane highway that used to bypass the city
of Houston from Katy to Pasadena, where I grew up,
is now 14-16 lanes wide in parts. It's traversed by
three giant looping highways that run in concentric
circles from the city center, only one of which, the
smallest, —the *610 Loop*—even existed when I was
a boy. Inside these expanding concrete rings on the
west side were major business development
centers, retail shopping, restaurants, and houses,
lots and lots of houses. While I marveled directly at
the city's expansion driving on its west side, the
growth was nearly matched on every point of the
compass extending from the city's center. Driving
across the metropolis Houston area would take
nearly two hours in clear traffic.

People have been attracted to the Houston
area for many reasons, none of which include the
weather, over the last 40 years, and 6.5 million
diverse people have spread themselves over a
5,500 square mile suburban-infused metropolis.
Meandering through this expansive, and genuinely
flat, urban landscape are several muddy creeks and
bayous that lazily drain from the coastal prairie land
upon which the city was built into Galveston Bay. On
their way, the waters mix with the brackish waters
from the tidal pull of the Gulf of Mexico. These
natural waterways have been incorporated into the
city's flood management program along with several
retention areas in an effort to fight the constant battle
that Houston has with the tropical rains that
occasion the city annually. These bayous and

reservoirs are central to many of the beautiful parks throughout Houston, including my favorite park, Frankie Carter Randolph Park, where Clear Creek begins its muddy passage into the city of Friendswood, south of Houston, where I make my home.

Now, Clear Creek is to *clear* as Loup City is to *city*—both apparently part of the same deceptive naming convention—and it winds its silty way through Friendswood from north to south on its way to League City where it meets with the equally misnamed *Clear* Lake. Clear Lake is less of a lake than the connecting point for several area creeks and bayous draining into Galveston Bay, and ultimately into the great Gulf of Mexico. Like the other waterways throughout the city, Clear Creek was soon going to be tested by Harvey. We all were, I suppose. But as I crossed the bridge over the creek before the turn into my neighborhood, its brown waters moved almost undetectably slow, far below the bridge and comfortably hugged by its banks.

I was elated to be back, and the familiar smell of home as I walked in the door greeted me with a relaxing breath. I started going through the thousand work emails that had accumulated in my days off, while I waited for everyone else to arrive. There was no thought given to a relaxing jog at Frankie Carter Randolph Park as afternoons in late August in the Houston area—between mosquitoes, humidity, and temperatures—are to be passed strictly indoors in the comfort of the always running air-conditioner. I had plenty of reading to keep me busy while I anxiously awaited Dedra and the kids. For me there was an excitement brought on by a long journey's end and the finale of my vacation. For everyone else, it was Wednesday.

"Oh excellent, you're home. You can take Grace to soccer practice," Dedra welcomed me scrambling to get in the door with her briefcase, a stack of papers from one or several of our kids' schools, and a bag that contained her uneaten lunch across her shoulder. This was not an uncommon occurrence in her role as the school counselor for more than 800 students, but the newness of the school year made it seem more hectic by comparison to the now-ended summer.

In such a state, I suppose it was a little much to expect her to greet me with "So, honey, how was your existential journey to look at the sun?" But it was at least clear from her entry that my return *was* welcome, if at least for my ability to assist with logistics. That was good enough for me. This was the kids' first full week of school and second week or so of fall sports activities. The annual re-establishment of routines after the long summer break was well underway, but not yet refined, particularly since I had been absent for the last five days. It's not a particularly easy transition in the first instance, but plugging an existential adventure into the calculus made it all the more complicated.

It was Wednesday, so there was both soccer and baseball practice in opposite directions—it was a two-car job, and my second car had arrived just in time. We took the kids to practice, got dinner, and made sure the kids had finished, or were working on, their homework. My ability to serve as a resource for homework questions had long since deteriorated in any topic with the exception of history or language arts, and even there my points were often rejected as inconsistent with the prevailing notions of their teacher or teenage expectations. I'm no longer ashamed to admit that I operate on a seventh grade level in mathematics, so now I simply urge the children to study the *magic* so they do not have to suffer like their father in ignorance. Thusly, I prodded them, negotiating disputes between them as they arose over precious resources such as jelly fruit snacks and erasers. Dedra was working to make sure the laundry cycle stayed in its constant motion and attended to the workload produced by her own school's first week. And so it was we spent Wednesday, hastening in blurry routines. While Harvey was growing on the radar, he was still flying under ours.

He was on mine Thursday though. The morning news programs were beginning to raise potential concerns for Harvey's impact. I watched the news with more interest than normal as I engaged in my customary morning routines to ensure the kids are getting ready for school. This generally involves my singing until they are up and out of bed. I don't recall my selection that morning, often I like to tie it to the day of the week or something happening at school or work. Occasionally, it will be a song of my

own lyrical composition, set to a favorite tune and
carried off acapella to such reviews as "Shut up!"
"Stop!" and "You're soooo annoying, I hate you!" But
you can't let the critics keep you from doing
something you love. With this resilient spirit, I roused
them to begin their day. I watched the TV in passing
as they got ready for school, and I mapped out the
plan for my day, which was still part of my vacation
time.

"Looks like there won't be any soccer game
or baseball *this* weekend," I informed them as they
got ready. "It looks like this storm is going to come
into Texas."

"Is it going to hit us?" Grace asked.

"It's not clear yet, but it looks like it is going to
hit Corpus Christi, which is south of us. That would
mean we still get a lot of rain." As a native of the Gulf
Coast, the concept of the *dirty side* of a tropical
storm is very much considered common knowledge.
Being on the northeast side of a hurricane is the
worst possible location as the rain bands circulate
counter clockwise around the center of the storm,
building as they tighten their circulation around the
center. Even if Harvey didn't move toward us, we
were likely to get enough rain in the weekend to
make fields unplayable. Our two athletes weren't
happy at the prospect of not having their games, so I
didn't let on that I was at least somewhat relieved I
didn't have to drive all the way across town where
they were to be played.

I had a lunch meeting in town with a couple

of former colleagues, and decided I would go for a workout in the morning beforehand so I didn't have to worry about squeezing it in during the evening, when an unforeseen errand might force it off the schedule. I tried to visit Frankie Carter Randolph Park at least a few times a week to exercise and generally avoid the rest of the world. Jogging its wooded trails along Clear Creek was a serene escape from the demands imposed upon me outside its boundaries.

It was on this jog, perhaps by virtue of the introspective mood I'd been lulled into on my vacation journey, that I first gave real consideration to Harvey. His position in the Gulf would almost certainly mean a landfall that would have some impact on Houston. What would Harvey bring? They were projecting very heavy rains. He was still a tropical storm at the time, so he didn't look like he was going to bring the brute force storm surge or winds that came with Hurricane Ike, which made landfall in nearby Galveston nearly ten years previously. We left town before Ike made landfall, but that was a much larger storm and was bringing with it a near-record storm surge. Harvey, on the other hand, was just going to bring rain. I can handle rain.

You can tell how long someone has been a Houstonian by asking them about their first hurricane. For me, it was Hurricane Alicia in 1983. It was August when that storm hit, too. Alicia was a direct hit on the city of Houston. Its winds blew out windows in the skyscrapers downtown; huge panes of glass popped out of buildings and tumbled hundreds of feet to the streets below, leaving wakes of office papers and supplies wafting down in the pouring rain behind them. It was a major disaster for the city. I was 15 years old.

  At our house, I slept the rock-like sleep of a teenage boy until my father woke me up to gather in the family room downstairs. "How could you sleep through *that*?" He shouted to me above the wail of the storm winds outside and the loud banging of a flailing decorative, tall fir against my window. Once the situation was presented to me, I had no idea how I could have slept through it (and only wished I retained the same depth of slumber now). Regardless, the contrast from deep sleep to the loud whistling winds of the storm was one that I would never forget.

  Following my father downstairs, we waited out the storm together as a family for hours, the howling wind wrought fear in our hearts with its incessancy. Our front door blew open in the mini vortex created by our tightly enclosed front porch. My father and I had to nail it shut to keep it from blowing open again and again. Two significantly tall trees in our front yard toppled, victims of Alicia's high winds. Time moved slowly as we listened intensely for the sound of a freight train lurking in the high-pitched moans of the constant gale. Tornadoes were our greatest fear, and I recall the constant worry that I might not be able to hear one amongst the general din until it was too late.

Against the Storm

Yet, with all of this danger around us, the most memorable moment for our entire family came as our minds were lulled into a quiet meditation on the hypnotic wind. My little sister sat atop my mother's lap, secured in her arms, and blissfully unaware of the Texas-sized cockroach making its way up her leg. When her peaceful state was interrupted by the realization that the tickling sensation she felt on her thigh was a 2½-inch long tree roach, the fear of the moment brought the full attention of all of our senses back to bear. It was a shriek, wrapped inside a scream, tuned to a volume level unrivaled by any stereo system of the day, and delivered with the high-pitched stab of an icepick to the ear drum. She flailed her body about as if she were a marionette being yanked violently from the stage by an invisible puppeteer; the cockroach taking flight from her spastic leg and onto the floor of the candle lit room. It quickly scurried under the couch and evaded our detection. For the rest of the storm, as we sat huddled in the candle-lit room, I kept a steady eye on the baseboard crevice the cockroach found to escape us, worried that I too might suffer the same encounter.

I don't care what my father said, there is *no way* that thing was more scared of us than we were of it. Lisa's scream channeled all of our tension into a single voice, and I remember it to this day as the defining moment of the storm itself, even though it was the least dangerous thing we were facing at the time. Eventually, the storm passed; we stretched and moved beyond our temporary shelter; and we replanted our upended trees. We fixed other minor damage scattered about the house. Ultimately, I was left with the sounds of Alicia etched in my memory and an irrational fear of cockroaches.

I've seen other storms, of course, some more memorable than others. They are simply a part of living on the *third coast.* Every storm leaves its own mark, I suppose. I chuckled as I thought about it on my jog, which had slowed to a brisk walk. The passage of time had softened the harder edges of the experience, and *survivor's glory* gave an almost nostalgic air to its memory. Alicia was a category 3 storm, and by comparison Harvey offered nothing at the time that would suggest he was somehow more worrisome that the major storm I'd survived as a boy. By the time I had finished my workout, I had resolved to meet Harvey head-on, riding out whatever he may bring.

I began the week by staring into the sun, and I would end it by staring into the eye of the storm.

III. Be Prepared

It was time to dust off the old Boy Scout in me. Preparation is the key to survival in a disaster, or in a corporate board room or courtroom for that matter, the situations being equally treacherous. I'd advanced to the level of Life Scout in the Boy Scouts as a teenager before abandoning spending weekends in nature for the prospects of hanging out in the city with friends who were disinclined to become members of the scouting organization. Nevertheless, I at least came away from my experience having learned the motto and how to tie a pretty good square knot. I would use my day off to prepare for whatever the storm had to offer. Challenge accepted, Harvey.

I met my former colleagues Scott and John for lunch in the heart of the city, between Buffalo Bayou and Braes Bayou, two central watersheds that would soon be facing the same challenge, albeit unwillingly. The three of us discussed, as we normally would at that time of year, the upcoming prospects of our college football teams, either feigning despair or giving way to hope beyond reason. They were both attorneys in private practice in a large downtown Houston law firm, and we had worked together for several years. Envious as they were of the concept of vacation, which I, as an *in-house* lawyer, was privileged enough to receive, they asked me about my road trip. I gave them an abbreviated version of the journey, sans the philosophical musings, but couldn't resist closing with my bit about the eye of the sun and the storm. From that point, we shifted our conversation to reminisce on other storms we had experienced.

They were not native Houstonians, and their first major storm recollection was Tropical Storm Allison. Allison forever dispelled the notion that a *mere* tropical storm was incapable of delivering destruction on the scale of a full-fledged hurricane. Allison dumped record-shattering rains across the Houston area, flooding Interstate 10 through the city such that only the tops of semi-trailer trucks were visible. The aerial photos of the floods stunned the nation. Flood waters pouring into the world's largest medical center destroyed electrical systems and billions of dollars of biomedical research being conducted in basement labs. Patients were tended to by heroic staff, *hand-bagging* ventilator patients so that they could survive a transfer in the utter chaos of the storm. The underground tunnel system that connects the many skyscrapers in downtown Houston was inundated, damaging many businesses. The impact on the city was widespread and catastrophic in many places. The rains that came from Allison exist in local lore. Everyone who lived in the city has stories of Allison, and we shared the three of ours with the same nostalgic aura that enveloped me on my morning jog.

It is here that I believe our combined recollections led me to adopt a faulty premise in my decision-making process. I succumbed to the tendency to believe that the most spectacular weather event in my life would be *the* most spectacular weather event for the rest of my life. Allison was the measuring stick by which all subsequent rain events were judged. Houston has experienced several flood events since, including two significant ones in the last few years. Yet, even after those floods, water cooler conversations would invariably proceed along these lines:

"Boy, that was an awful flood in [insert Houston community affected] yesterday. I saw they got 18 inches of rain. Terrible stuff. Nothing like Allison, of course."

"Of course. Yeah, Allison, that was a terrible storm. I remember...."

Allison was the upper limit in my imagination for rainfall. I watched it myself from my porch on the banks of Chigger Creek, which ran directly behind my then back yard, 15-20 feet below. My home sat atop what was effectively the levy for my old neighborhood in Friendswood, protecting all of the homes on the other side from the rain-fueled swelling of Chigger Creek. It rained harder for longer during Allison than I can ever remember. It was torrential. The creek swelled to engulf my back yard and work its way up the levy until it was nearly flush with my patio floor when finally the rains relented. Like the rest of the city, I was paralyzed by the rising waters, but unlike many others, I was dry.

Amazingly, the waters stopped rising just soon enough to ensure that my personal property was spared in the nick of time. I recalled a Hollywood-esque ending to my already time-softened memory of Allison's dreadful wrath upon the Houston area, at least as I considered it from my personal perspective. Their stories of escaping serious damage to their homes, and the humorous reflections of their challenges further distanced from my reflection from the true nature of the storm. The anxieties of the experiences of Allison were tamped down by time, and by "knowing how the story ended," in the same way that led to my envy of Zach's time in college. Our lunch conversation only heightened my confidence in riding out Harvey.

As we spoke, and as if strengthened by my own will to oppose him, Harvey churned. The warm waters of the Gulf of Mexico were more than ample fuel for Harvey's preparation. That once ordinary mass of clouds in the southern Gulf had formed into a rapidly evolving storm that now bore the status of *hurricane*. Hurricane Harvey marched closer to the coast, gaining strength with each passing moment. Nothing in the skies or seas was poised to stop his continued growth. It was now only a matter of time before our wills would collide. And the clock was ticking.

I casually finished my lunch and bid my friends the best of luck in their own storm preparation. It was Boy Scout time now! I had to get some paper and office supplies for the home office on my way back from lunch, so I used the stop to begin the accumulation of survival supplies. It is often overlooked that office supply stores stock bottles of water for business' needs. I felt this would give me an optimal location to secure water in case fear-inspired runs at the local grocery store had exhausted their supplies. While this was somewhat worst-case-scenario thinking on my part, perhaps bordering on paranoia, I felt it necessary to my whole mindset of survival preparation. Try to think of the worst situation, and plan for it. Avoid surprises. One does not rise to the level of Life Scout by making presumptions in preparation.

I picked up the requisite water provisions, some AA batteries under the same theory as the water reserves, and a Sharpie. Sharpies are always useful. It was entirely likely we had a drawer full of Sharpies in our kitchen desk at home, given that the notion of needing to pick up a Sharpie is almost always on my mind when I walk into the office supply store. Regardless, redundancy was another key principle in my preparation process. A Life Scout would never jump from a plane with only one parachute—a back-up is always necessary. If we had some water and batteries already at the house, we would now have even more—and a fresh means to label them.

Having a grandfather and uncle who worked (and work) for NASA my entire childhood and adult life likely had as much to do with my preparation mindset as my Life Scout training. I certainly remember the concept of redundancies from tours of the Johnson Space Center with my grandfather as a child. They are among my fondest memories. The life support systems and flight control systems of spacecraft that they worked on were designed such that the failure of one important component would have a back-up capable of handling the necessary task. The scientific approach to developing procedures for addressing the gross multitude of known and unknown problems presented by manned-space flight was imbued, albeit at a substantially diluted level, to my own psyche.

Tom Hanks made famous a line from the movie *Apollo 13* for which nearly everyone knows our city's name: "*Houston, we have a problem.*" Slightly misquoted, the line is tossed around ubiquitously and humorously to describe difficult situations of varying degrees. Yet, its fame is derived from the real men and women who put together the solution to bring those astronauts home safely. My grandfather collaborated with many others at NASA to solve the problems faced by the astronauts on the Apollo 13 mission, and it was an experience that affected him so deeply that he wrote a letter to his family in order to ensure that they would know what it meant to him, and what they too could strive to achieve. He wrote: "…Our family has been a part of a great adventure and I hope, when you are grown, you can be a part of a noble cause such as Project Apollo.…You live in a remarkable time, use all your energy to be prepared to participate in it."

My uncle reminded me on Monday that my grandfather had passed away on August 21, 2003,

14 years to the day before the solar eclipse I had just witnessed. Whether by coincidence or grand design (if there be any difference in the two), this had the effect of keeping my grandfather close at mind throughout the week. The immediate byproduct of this being a heightened awareness of his problem-solving advice in my preparation process.

I proceeded from the office supply store to the grocery store near our house, where I decided I would find whatever good canned food and other useful items remained on the shelves. I listened to the news on the drive back into Friendswood in between my musical selections. Harvey's efforts at intensification matched my own. It appeared he was heading for a landfall just north of Corpus Christi. It wasn't exactly clear what would happen from that point according to the experts, but it seemed certain that we would receive very heavy rain, with flooding likely.

To a Houstonian the phrase "very heavy rain with flooding likely" is not particularly unusual or cause for significant concern. Heavy rains visit the city from time to time with flooding and roads closures affecting dozens of homes and bogging the city down for a day or so. In fact, in the last couple of years there were a couple of "100-year flood events" in Houston – the Tax Day Flood and Memorial Day Flood. They were damaging to the people affected, including a friend of mine who lost his vehicle to rising waters in his driveway. But they were not extremely widespread and did not affect my little corner of the world. Moreover, of course, they were nothing like Allison, the upper limit of rainfall possibilities. So, the news reports of rain also did nothing to raise doubt in my decision to ride out Harvey.

My visit to the grocery store went better than expected. Rather than post-apocalyptic scene I had envisioned, it was a relatively normal afternoon at the grocery store (or so I presumed, as this was not my normal grocery shopping time). I saw some barren shelves and some mild chaos but only by virtue of a previously planned store remodeling (or rearranging as the case may be). I barely had the HEB layout down as it was and they were changing it on me. I wandered around the store finding different items in my normal traffic patterns and was lured frequently by the sheer expectation of location into purchasing multiple products. It was a brilliantly subtle marketing strategy, and I would have given it more appreciation had it not also resulted in dragging out my search for bean dip.

This is where the Life Scout training kicked back in. Bean dip was the go-to protein source, along with Spam, as I remember from my boyhood scouting camping trips. Eagle Scouts obviously receive superior survivor training skills, but bean dip has never let me down as an emergency food supply. Apparently, the community is relatively filled with Life Scouts, as my bean dip expedition yielded only five cans, two of which were jalapeño flavored and unlikely to be popular with anyone other than myself. I got them, of course, knowing that I would at least be ensured of two cans of bean dip once the rationing process cycled out. The bean dip was strategically positioned near several jars of salsa. Being Houstonian, salsa was generally my primary source of vegetable consumption, and it seemed a natural emergency ration complement to the protein offered by the bean dip. I had to compliment HEB on their new stocking arrangement.

I gathered several other provisions and returned home in time to greet the kids as they got home from school. There was a surprising degree of normalcy to their pace and post-school routines. Though, I suppose I would have had the same demeanor had I been subject to my typical work-a-day schedule. But I was on vacation. And I had put it to good use.

"Why do we have all this water?" Grace mused quizzically as she walked by the stacks of water bottles lined up against the living room wall.

"Emergency provisions. Getting ready for Hurricane Harvey," I replied with a barely muted excitement. The provision shopping had stoked the embers sparked by my morning jog. The game was afoot!

"Yeah, but I don't think we will need *that* much water."

"Gallon a day. Per person. 3 days. Minimum," I barked off as if reciting from a procedure manual. "I probably should get more, to be honest."

"Are we having a party?" She was rifling

through the bags with bean dip and salsa. And chips —the obvious and necessary delivery vehicle for the bean dip and salsa, which also was conveniently shelved adjacent to the emergency protein and vegetables.

"No, no party. Those are just emergency food supplies." She had not been into scouting as a child, though we had gone on a number of family camping trips. In any event, I could scarce fault her woeful lack of survival preparation awareness.

"*Beer*? Beer is an emergency food supply?" The skepticism in her tone rang louder than her voice. It triggered my own internal concerns that my shopping had been inspired as much by my youthful non-scouting experiences as by my Life Scout training.

"Ok, well, the beer is not *necessarily* an emergency item, but I don't want to discount its importance. Look, we're not having a party. Just getting ready for the storm. We'll have a family meeting at dinner and can talk about it."

"Oh yay. Family meeting." Her skepticism had been replaced by an even stronger sarcasm. Family meetings were generally called to address concerns rising from any member of the family, but often involved parental lecturing of one kind or another. In a house full of teenagers, you can imagine their popularity.

This family meeting topic, however, was quite popular as the excitement of a coming storm and now expected day off from school on Friday fueled a vibe that was in tune with my enthusiastic spirit of preparation. The kids rallied to search the house and gather various items—chargers, batteries, flashlights, etc.—into the living room so that we could inventory our supplies. Dedra joined them in their gatherings, but her spirit was not in tune with the same anticipatory vibe.

Dedra's dislike for the prospect of a tropical storm equaled or exceeded her anxiety relating to the growth of biological pathogens in improperly stored foods. She wanted nothing to do with Harvey. My preparations had offered her no comfort, particularly as the weather news talked up the strengthening of now Hurricane Harvey. Harvey's own preparation continued incessantly, churning stronger and stronger still. Possibly a category 2 when it makes landfall they said. That was enough in Dedra's mind to activate the Etzel Family Evacuation Plan.

It was the most sensible option, but it was complicated by the fact that the path to our shelter in the hills of central Texas, her parent's home in Hondo, was in the direct line of the storm. Her parent's prior house in New Braunfels sheltered us securely during Hurricane Ike. Their Hondo home would have been ideal were it not that Harvey appeared headed in their general direction. She also had relatives, her brother Dwayne's family and her Aunt Dorothy's family, in Dallas, due north and away from the path of the storm. They would welcome us for sure.

Once again, it was difficult to assail her logic. But her years of counseling training would certainly have helped her realize that I was making my *hunker-down* decision based in an emotional context brought upon by my own eclipse-induced introspection. I knew in my rational brain that it didn't matter that our current house was untouched by Allison or that it did not appear that we would be directly hit by the highest winds of Harvey. Dedra offered a near-fail safe plan to avoid facing the storm. It was the optimal choice. Yet, something compelled me to stay with the house, to face the storm as I had convinced myself all day. For purposes of lore, I'd like it to be known that my words were, "I'd rather die in my home in Houston than evacuate to Dallas!"

But if I were forced to be honest, it went nothing like that. We both recognized she was making the wise decision, but that something from afar had called me on a fool's errand.

I now had the duty to convince the troops whom I had just stirred into a frenzy for battle that they had been called to fall back to safer ground for the long weekend, while their commander held down the fort on his own. Recognizing that with the fool often lies adventure, they resisted the new orders with varying degrees of protest. I had, it seemed, created a bit of a situation. We debated the topic calmly, once the initial remonstrations were culled, and came to no satisfactory conclusion before deciding that it was best to sleep on it and decide in the morning.

In the meantime, we checked the plans of family and friends. My mother and sisters were staying in place in the Pasadena and Bellaire areas, respectively. Other friends, like my friend Toby whose vehicle fell victim to the Tax Day flood two years ago, were heading to higher ground with family out of town. I coordinated communication plans with my staff at work, which would likely soon switch to emergency operation status. Harvey had our full attention, and we spent the restless night questioning our plans.

The morning brought news that Harvey was not suffering from any doubts of his own. Impervious to our mortal need for sleep, Harvey lost little steam in the muggy warm nights in the Gulf of Mexico. He was stronger than expected and showing no signs of relenting before crashing into the coast somewhere to our southwest. This early morning forecast certainly offered additional support for the evacuation plan approach, and we decided that Dedra and the twins would make their way to Dallas after lunch, before the rains began to move ashore in our area. Alex, as the oldest offspring in the homestead, would remain with me to provide any assistance I may need, "Take care of your father," I believe were the specific instructions from his mother. From the twins' somewhat disgruntled perspective, he had become the beneficiary of additional video game time, and the activities they were offered in return did not seem to account them fairly. Like most compromises, it was generally disliked. But Dallas offered a safe outpost for them and had the side benefit in increasing the duration of the full ration period for Alex and me. I originally had concerns that I had not established sufficient redundancy in the water and bean dip supplies, and those fears were alleviated with the split plan approach.

Though displeased at what they considered *missing out,* Grace and Harrison assisted me in putting the patio furniture and grill into the garage while Alex gathered pool toys and other potential back yard projectiles. Alex had just recovered from a broken wrist, his cast being removed earlier in the week, and he was limited in heavy lifting in his duties by doctor's orders. The supply gathering initiative of the previous night had shown that we were generally in pretty good shape with regard to food, water, charger cords, first aid kits, and Sharpies, but our flashlight collection was, in my estimation, inadequate. I used the morning to make a last run to the grocery store to see if I could find a flashlight and some dry ice—Chuck's dry ice had lasted nearly four days in the cooler, and I thought it an excellent option for extending our refrigeration capacity during any power outage. I found no decent options for traditional hand-held flashlights, being that I was now on the back-side of the community preparation curve, so I opted for a head-band light. It reminded me of the lights coal miners wear on their helmets or the ones doctors wear in surgery. In any event, it was better than any other option available, and I picked it up as my last preparation item.

With the addition of the headband light, our preparation was complete. I was ready for Harvey. And he was certainly ready for me. As the clock ticked on Friday, Harvey rapidly intensified, ultimately into a strong category 4 hurricane. Rockport, Texas, was in line for the direct hit sometime late that night. The stage was set. The challenge was about to begin. We put our plans in motion and packed the twins and Dedra off for a long weekend in Dallas while Alex and I stayed with the house.

We hugged our goodbyes, and the rain began to fall.

IV. The Rain Comes

The rain came. Not much at first. Certainly
nothing that would cause a Houstonian to bat an
eye. Dedra and the twins would be on the north side
of Houston before the rains really would hit us here
on the south side in Friendswood, if we had timed it
right. They were taking with them our newly acquired
vehicle. So new, in fact, that it was in the grace
period for transferring the insurance from our
previous car to the newly acquired one. With
confidence that a claims denial would be
manufactured from such a situation, they took the
new, albeit pre-owned, car to the safety of their
Dallas shelter. We remained with the Honda Pilot
(typically Dedra's primary vehicle) and my old, trusty
FJ Cruiser, the car I had been driving for the last 10
years. The FJ Cruiser had 210,000 miles on it now,
and by any account, had seen its better days. But it
can get through just about anything, and has
powered all sorts of accessories on outdoor trips
with its AC outlet in the back. It was to be our
emergency generator if we lost power and needed to
charge our phones in order to maintain
communication. It had been through its share of
flood waters before, sitting high enough off the
ground to traverse lightly flooded streets. I viewed it
as our tried and true lifeboat.

I spent the afternoon and early evening
catching up on emails from work and cooking up
some spaghetti. I decided I would start eating as

much of our quarter cow as possible before the power ran out and the dry ice evaporated. I would begin with some of the ground beef for spaghetti that night, and use the stew meat for an "all-day simmer" chili the next day, and move to the steak cuts when power was lost and I had to resort the charcoal grill for food preparation. I had purchased enough charcoal to grill for three weeks. I suppose the prospect of grilling food daily for survival purposes excited me as much as it would any weekend grill enthusiast. Life Scouts are always at the ready around the camp fire.

In the midst of my meal planning, I was pleasantly interrupted by a Fed Ex delivery driver. Harvey's rains had not yet interfered with Houston's commerce in any substantial manner, and the delivery man met me at the door with a large box. It was from Napa, California. Dedra had recently returned from a girl's trip to Napa, touring various vineyards and falling for several wine-sales pitches. She returned from her trip with a few bottles of wine in her suitcases and the promise of several more to follow by mail. I viewed the timing of the delivery as nothing less than divine recognition—a symbolic gift from Harvey himself to toast the beginning of our adversarial contest. A light rain danced rhythmically on the sidewalk below the deliveryman's feet, as if the drops were peaceful ambassadors announcing the imminent arrival of a steadily marching foe. Perhaps this was Harvey's way of offering one last chance for a peaceful surrender and evacuation. But I had already made my choice to stay. I decided to face the storm. I signed for the package as if to acknowledge the acceptance of my fate.

Whatever that fate would be, it would at least be accompanied with a good glass of wine. The spaghetti simmered. I periodically turned to the TV to check the latest on Harvey, which was bearing down on the coast with tremendous winds and rains. It looked like its path could stall after it made landfall and its slow movement might result in dropping 20+ inches of rainfall in the Houston area after destroying any building not ready to survive 130+ MPH winds in Rockpork. Harvey was going to leave a heavy footprint on Texas, that was becoming clear. How heavy was the only question that remained.

It was Friday night, normally family movie night, but it felt quite like a Saturday, perhaps due to the kids being off from school. Indeed, it is at about this time that that my sense of the days of the week had been lost completely. I would soon begin referring to days as *the day before* or *the day after* a certain event, like some pre-calendar age ancestor. But I suppose that is to be expected when you're locked in a battle with nature itself. The natural world acknowledges no days of the week. Only daylight hours and nighttime hours. As that particular day gave way into night, the rain fell harder with the darkness, though it was still not falling at any rate that would pose a concern.

The Astros were playing a late game on the West Coast, so I thought I would stay up to watch the game and catch up on them a bit. I had not really been able to follow them over the last week or so, due to my out-of-state vacation and the preparation for the storm. They were safe and dry in Anaheim that night, facing the Angels in the midst of a dreadful August of baseball; well, at least when compared to the utterly remarkable first half of their season. The Astros 2017 season began with record-setting statistical numbers on offense and a winning percentage that was among the highest in a baseball history spanning more than 100 years. They had run so far away from their opponents in their division of the American League that they were virtually assured of a position in the playoffs at the beginning of August.

However, *virtually assured* is not the same as *mathematically assured,* and a seven-game losing streak in early August began to worry those who were once confident in the dictates of the virtual world. José Altuve, the Astros's superstar second baseman, was mired in his worst batting slump of the year after a start that brought back references to the immortal baseball legend Ted Williams. Altuve broke the Houston Astros's records for the number of hits by a player during a single month of the season in the month of July. While it may not jump out at first, it is a truly remarkable feat given the Astros played five *fewer* games that month than any other month (due to the three-day All Star Game break and two other normal days off). He had more hits in a month than anybody in Astros history and he did it with 17% fewer games! His remarkable feats were shared by guys like George Springer (who, as late as July, was batting nearly .500 with runners in scoring position and two outs—clutch hitting numbers only rivaled by my children on video games). A whole host of contributors made the Astros the most potent lineup the league had seen in nearly 100 years.

On top of that, their pitchers were absolutely dealing it. Dallas Keuchel had begun the season in Cy Young award candidate form, winning nine games and losing none. The rest of the starters and bullpen were solid, if not exceptional. But Keuchel suffered an injury in June that left the staff without its Ace for more than a month. His return in August gave evidence that he was still working through the injury, as he lost two straight games and his earned-run average for the month was over five. In short, August brought doubt.

Their fortunes seemed to mirror my own. After a great early summer, August presented to our household three emergency room trips, a minor fracture, a mild concussion, and a totaled car. That's an outlier month even with four active teenagers. And it wasn't over yet. Like the Astros, I was sitting and waiting for the storm without my Ace. Having been an Astros fan from the time I was the smallest of boys, it was perhaps easy to make this connection. It was also easy to doubt. I'd seen some really great teams in my lifetime, witnessing great pitching aces like Mike Scott, Nolan Ryan, Roy Oswalt, and the near immortal, albeit shorter-termed performances of Randy Johnson and Roger

Clemens. The Astros have had great players like José Cruz, Kevin Bass, Glenn Davis, Jeff Bagwell, Ken Caminiti, Lance Berkman, and my all-time favorite player, Craig Biggio. The list could go on and on, as the Astros have their fair share of great baseball players. Yet, in all those players' glorious seasons and with all their stardom, it was never quite enough. Each season revealed one better team, one unlucky break, one twist of fate. So you can't fault an old Houston Astros fan for harboring a degree of doubt even in the best of times. When the month of August brought more losses than it did wins, the doubt of the season beyond September was in full bloom. My expectations subject to such cautions, I turned to the Astros game looking, like the rest of my city I presumed, for a distraction from the storm.

Alex came through the living room to check on the status of things.

"Astros are on. Late game against the Angels," I informed him succinctly.

He grabbed a bottle of water from one of the packages along the wall, and made his way to the couch.

"Whoa there, big fella, don't drink from the emergency water supply!" I blurted out upon witnessing a gross violation of preparation protocol.

"I thought these were for your hurricane party thingy. Haven't we started that?" he replied.

"It's not a hurricane party. They're not party supplies. They're emergency food and water provisions. We could be without power and water for a couple days, maybe more," I chided parentally.

"Couple of *days*!? There's enough water here to last until December," he retorted in the charming manner that teenagers maintain in conversations in which they believe they know better than their parents. So, generally, every conversation.

"It's less than you think, Water Waster," I replied in a jokingly scolding manner. "You need a gallon a day to drink. Now, with Mom and the twins gone, we're probably in pretty good shape."

"I'd say we're in *real* good shape."

"Well, the point is, the sink is currently fully operational. As is the refrigerator door dispenser. Both offering perfectly drinkable water that is not part of the emergency supply stores," I responded in overly pedantic manner.

"Well, I've already opened it. So, I'll just drink one less when the Apocalypse comes. Is there more spaghetti?"

I decided not to make a federal case of the insubordination, on account that he had likely adjudged the amount of our water supplies accurately. He went to get himself another serving of spaghetti, where he spotted the open bottle of wine next to the pot.

"You're drinking *wine*? I thought you said it wasn't a party?" His tone dripped with sarcasm.

"It's NOT a party!" I snapped back, more sharply than he deserved, as much for the insubordination as for the fact that he had made the same comment as Grace. I responded, defensively, "It's Saturday night; I am entitled as an adult to enjoy wine on my couch watching a baseball game. In fact, as a parent of four teenage children, I would argue that it is medically necessary."

"Well, you're cooking spaghetti, there's all this wine, snacks, the Astros game is on. Seems like a party. A very lame party, I grant you that, but a party nonetheless." He filled his plate and sat back down to watch the game.

"Why are the Astros sucking so much right now?" he said this as if in casual conversation.

"Well, it's a long season. We've had some injuries. So, it's just a slump. We'll be okay in September," I replied not wanting him to share in the doubt that sought to infect my own outlook. The words I spoke were true in every way and certainly reflected my desired outcome. But did I still *believe* the words as I said them? Likewise, I had every confidence in my emergency preparations— regardless of how much they may, in some way, and with the fortuitous timing of the wine delivery compounding—reflect those of a party. But for the Astros and me, the August storm had come. How confident could I be?

I flipped back and forth between the game and stations with various weather reporters standing outside in the middle of a now category 4 storm to furnish information provided to them by machines and people in dry and secure places. Yet, I was compelled to watch it. I suppose many people are. We want to see the reporter standing in the storm, as if he or she is fighting it for us in some disconnected way. I marveled at the winds behind the reporter bending trees and street signs, though I do not recall what station he was on or where in the storm's path he was standing.

"Do you think they'll cancel school again on Monday?" Alex asked.

"For purposes of any homework that is currently due on Monday, I would plan on having school. For purposes of water ration consumption, I would plan on being off on Monday and maybe Tuesday."

"Sounds like you're trying to have it both ways there, Pops," he offered, to note what he considered my inconsistency.

"It's called planning. Preparation. You plan for the worst and hope for the best. Perfectly consistent, my lad," I responded in my parental pontificating tone. Perhaps he was correct on the volume of water, but I had him cornered on this one.

"Put it back on the Astros," he responded, acknowledging my argument point by changing the subject. Any parent could identify with the gratification gleaned from such silent victory.

The Astros were locked in a close, low-scoring game, the hits and runs from the early season highs were still evading them. They had scrapped to a 2-1 lead when George Springer snuck by on a wild pitch. Alex had fallen asleep on the couch. It was late, but the ninth inning was coming up, so I decided to top off my wine glass and finish the game. Ken Giles came in during the bottom of the ninth and closed out the victory.

"Yes!" I blurted out loudly to the TV on the final out. Alex rustled gently on the couch, but did not wake up. "It's not a party," I muttered softly to myself. I wandered off to bed with Harvey's rains providing a soothing rhythm as accompaniment. The Astros's narrow win and Harvey lulled me into the night's slumber, and I enjoyed my last full night's sleep for some time to come.

V. This Ain't No Party

The next morning greeted us with more rain. It was, by slight degrees, stronger than the rain from the day before. Monotonous, but still nothing too out of the ordinary. There was also more thunder, and I began to wonder when we would lose power. I began my *all-day chili* preparations with the hope that I'd be able to finish them on my electric stovetop. In the midst of my searing the stew meat, I received a call from my friend, Randy.

"Hey, are you guys still up for the party?" he asked in his usual upbeat tone.

"It's *not* a party! They're emergency food supplies, dammit!" I retorted exasperatedly.

"What?!" he sounded surprised at my rebuke. "I'm talking about the fight night party. The one my Grace and I asked you and Dedra about couple weeks ago." His fiancée, also named Grace, had indeed discussed the party with us at dinner a short while back. Floyd Mayweather, a champion boxer who had trouble keeping his punches within the confines of the ring, and Colin McGreggor, a mixed-martial arts fighter with a savvy marketing team, were scheduled to fight in a boxing match that was highly anticipated by many people. I was not one of those people, but it was an opportunity to hang out with friends and enjoy a Saturday night. So, we originally committed to joining the party. "Are y'all still coming?" he asked.

"Dude, you *are* aware that there is a hurricane blowing through our region right now, aren't you?"

"It's barely raining over here." He lived in Seabrook, another of the multitude upon multitude of suburban towns surrounding Houston, situated to the southeast of the city right between the banks of Galveston Bay and Clear Lake.

"Dedra and the twins left for Dallas yesterday. It's supposed to rain even harder later. There's no way, man," I said in a tone reserved for family members. We've known each other since we were in eighth grade, and I count him as a brother.

"Come on, man! Don't be a wuss!" Our long familiarity often gave way to one or the other of us resorting to eighth grade tactics for convincing the other to undertake one adventure or another. "You and Alex can make it. We've got sooooo much food over here, if you get stuck you will survive just fine!"

"I don't see it happening. I'll check the roads later this afternoon."

"Ted and Jim are coming." It was another go-to eighth grade convincing tactic, well played. I could see he was working all of the angles.

"Ted and Jim don't live 15 miles away, separated by Clear Creek," I responded.

"Come on. Remember that one storm we rode out here when we were in college? Where's that sense of adventure?" He went all-in with the nostalgia card, an obvious last-ditch effort to convince me to change my mind. It was an excellent tactic, and one that I myself resorted to frequently when I'm found in the role of convinc-*or* and not convinc-*ee.* He was alluding to another tropical storm—Allison—in 1989.

We were hanging out with a group of guys at our friend Chuck's (not my father-in-law Chuck's) family's house in Seabrook, which sat right affront Galveston Bay, when "Little Allison" blew in to town. It wasn't a major storm, but it had a big enough storm-surge to block off the low road connecting Chuck's house to the main roadway, Highway 146. We were stranded on the island that Chuck's house had become once the storm came ashore. At the storm's height, we heard what sounded like a heavy truck passing by and felt the sudden shift in air pressure even from inside the house. It was a frightening sound, but the presumed twister passed by us without damaging the house before we were able to react and scramble to the interior bathroom. Other than that single harrowing moment, *Little Allison* mostly brought just a long day or so of heavy rains.

We rode out the storm playing poker, drinking beer, and designing various other pranks and games as the time allowed—perhaps not entirely unexpected behavior from five 20-21 year old *men.* In that we were generally unaware of the existence of the storm until it came ashore, we had not adequately prepared for it. As the storm continued to push through, we discovered in the midst of our afternoon activities that our provisions were severely depleted. Randy, Chuck, and I volunteered for a mission to hike through the flooded streets to the convenience store on Highway 146 to obtain the emergency supplies necessary to sustain us for the remainder of the storm.

Given its proximity to Galveston Bay, the flood waters that separated Chuck's house from the convenience store were primarily caused by the surging storm tide. White caps peaked on the swells stirred up from the blowing wind. We would need to traverse a narrow roadway, flanked by deep ditches invisible under the floodwater, up the rise leading to the highway where the convenience store sat. It was not a particularly wise journey.

We made our way along the narrow road with the crests of white caps lapping our chest. We encountered rats displaced from nearby harbors swimming in the waters in search for dry ground. Despite the perils that faced us, we knew that the party's survival depended on us. After the half-mile wade, we arrived at the store, much to the delight of the owner-clerk who had not expected much business that day. We dripped with water as we made our way through the store to purchase three cases of beer, eight cans of bean dip, four bags of chips, and several candy bars. We slung the food bags over our arms and held the beer above our head, each of us resting one case atop our head as we made the treacherous journey back. Each of us almost lost our footing among the swells as we balanced our loads in the driving rain and sloshing water. But we made it back alive, and with enough supplies to ensure we would experience no want in our festivities.

Our youthful foolishness on that day was the stuff of lore and has been re-told, with varying degrees of accuracy, during many a get-together since. They were fond memories. Made particularly fonder by virtue of the fact that we did not die as victims of our own stupidity. It was just the kind of nostalgic thinking—20 plus years on—that had fueled my decision to stay and face Harvey where I was. Nevertheless, not even Randy's best *remember when we* story could convince me to double-down on my decision and take a journey across the southern side of the Houston metroplex to Seabrook. If anything, the recollections only caused me to question the originating source of the philosophical foundation upon which I had based my Harvey preparation strategy. Perhaps the recollections from my Life Scout training were not as strong as I thought.

"If I were 21 years old again, I would be on my way over now. But I think I'll play this one safer," I responded, and he relented. We gave way to a discussion of the Astros, another common topic between us. Despite the victory last night, he remained worried. The team continued to struggle to score runs. It was hard to argue with him, as much as I would have enjoyed it. As a longtime Astros fan, the *Houston doubt* was festering inside him as well.

"Well, if you change your mind, we'll be

here," he ended our conversation, and I returned to my chili.

As the day went on, the aroma of my all-day chili filled the downstairs; the spices and stew meat from our quarter cow wafted up from the kitchen like a burnt offering in an attempt to appease the storm I had challenged in my vanity. Yet as the chili's fragrance built, Harvey's rage only grew stronger, as if offended by my sacrifice (I suppose it may have been a little heavy on the red pepper, but otherwise I thought it quite good). It rained increasingly harder throughout the day, building to a crescendo in the late afternoon.

Indeed, at that time, to call it rain would not be accurate. Rain implies that there were *raindrops*. There were no drops. Only waves. Waves of water falling from the skies. The water pounded on the windows, not by the force of a blowing wind, but by the sheer mass of the water falling from the sky. It wasn't rain. It was as if Harvey were pounding us with his fists over and over again. It was a frightening barrage.

Our dog, Maggie, who had handled the preparation phase and storm build up without much interest, became increasingly anxious. She paced back and forth briskly, letting out an occasional bark toward the strange invader banging outside our window. I'm not sure how long it *rained* like that, to be honest. Time was suspended. Maggie and I were locked in a moment in time grasping with the uncomfortable reality of nature's power. If this *had* been a party, the party was over. I went upstairs to check on Alex.

I opened his door, "Are you seeing this rain?" he was not. He had his headphones on, talking with his friends while they roamed around a virtual landscape battling some enemy or another. He was as oblivious to the storm as I was when I slept through part of Hurricane Alicia at his age. I tapped him on the shoulder,

"Are you seeing this rain?" I repeated.

"Yeah, it's raining. So what?" His attention was not primarily focused on the weather outside.

"You don't hear it pounding on the window?"

"I'm in the middle of a game," he responded tersely.

"Well, this is kind of an emergency situation. We need to be on alert for possible tornados," I warned him paternally. "Downstairs is the safest place to be. My closet is a good interior shelter with pipes for the bathroom in one of its walls." As I counseled, the heaviest rain began to abate to something that would resemble a heavy thunderstorm—still strong, but at least discernible as rain.

"Ok, ok. Give me a minute," he was not really engaging me yet at the level of my emergency declaration. "Is the chili ready?"

"Yes, the chili is ready. But I am more concerned with our safety right now than dinner. Let's go downstairs. Promptly!" I stated with added emphasis. I really should mandate that the kids complete more emergency procedure training drills.

"My dad said there's a tornado. I've gotta go duck and cover, or whatever. Later," he reluctantly spoke into his mic and walked briskly by me on his way out the door.

"Technically, I didn't say there *was* a tornado, I said I was worried one may be lurking in this heavy storm," I said as he walked past me, the rain continuing to lessen outside as if to undermine my efforts at impressing Alex with the gravity of the situation. He would likely assume I was just stirring him from his room to have him unplug from video games—one of my frequent duties as the father of teenagers. Yet, I understood that the video games offered a distraction from the storm and the boredom of the isolation indoors. I also saw it as a valuable information source for local conditions. He and his friends could, and did, convey the status of the storm at their respective houses and streets within the Friendswood area, in the same manner I had been checking with my friends in other parts of Houston via text messages. The golden age of information has its benefits. But I knew the benefits of having access to all of that data would be sustained only so long as we kept power, and I was not expecting it to hang on much longer.

My phone had generally been tethered to the charger the entire afternoon in anticipation of such an outage. I checked it when we went downstairs. It contained alerts for flood warnings and tornado watches. I had received text messages from friends and from Dedra who was monitoring the storm from her secure location at her brother's house. Randy had texted to a group of our friends and was reporting that he had endured some strong rains, but there was no water in his yard or street. All systems were still go for his party, he was happy to report.

The rain had slowed to a sprinkle and the water that had accumulated during the immense downpour was draining quickly. I decided to take the lifeboat (FJ Cruiser) out on a reconnaissance mission to check on the status of the main roadways connecting Friendswood to Houston and Galveston. The ditches in the neighborhood and along the roads were swollen and rushing rapidly down their channels into the creeks in which they fed. I checked the crossing of Clear Creek under FM 528, a major seven-lane roadway connecting Friendswood to the Houston freeway system. It also happened to be the road connecting Friendswood to Seabrook and Randy's house, although that was incidental to my information gathering exercise.

Clear Creek was gorged with water and out of its banks. It looked more like a river flowing beneath the FM 528 bridge, though it *was* still *beneath* the passing by a few feet, making the road fully traversable. Water rushed from the roadway above to fuel the creek's rise as it quickly moved the rainwater through Friendswood and toward Galveston Bay.

I turned the FJ around and checked the

bridges over Chigger Creek and Cowards Creek, which traversed roads needed for my access north and south, respectively. Both creeks were out of their banks and closer to the base of their bridges than Clear Creek was on FM 528. This was not surprising as FM 528 is a significantly higher crossing. Those roads were holding, but it wasn't clear for how long as the run off from the volume of Harvey's initial volley continued to pour into the creeks from every direction. As my mission continued, the next band of Harvey's rains began to arrive.

That's how these storms hit you, one band after another, with lulls in between. Harvey was no different from other storms in that regard. But there was *something* about Harvey that wasn't the same. I rushed back home and parked the FJ in the back outside the garage door, then ran back into the house to check the news. The rates of rain that Harvey was producing were shocking to even the most experienced of weathercasters. Intense bands appeared to be bringing rain with rates of four to five inches per hour! They simply didn't know what to predict.

Harvey had been inland all day, and had weakened to a tropical storm, but he was ambling around like a drunken octogenarian along the southeast Texas coastline. The center of the storm drifted slowly and aimlessly while its rain bands spiraled around the center lashing the areas to the northeast of its eye (i.e., the dirty side). Houston took each blow. The effect was rainfall that was concerning the weathercasters, and their tones were dramatic. They were creating new colors for their rainfall maps to project rates and accumulation amounts that hitherto only existed in imagination. Parts of Houston were already experiencing flooding, with no sign that Harvey was prepared to relent.

The weather reports had killed any lingering notion of any attempt to join the fight-night party despite continued updates from Seabrook that the roadways nearby were clear, and the rain was light. Harvey's current meanderings kept the heaviest rain bands just to the west of Seabrook. However, I lived just to the west of Seabrook. The fight party was a no-go.

We would settle for chili and the Astros game —with a nice Cabernet, of course. The Astros jumped to an early 5-1 lead, showing signs that the bats may be coming to life. Outside, Harvey began to flail us again with walls of water lashing mighty blows against the house. It was beyond my recollection of the hardest Allison ever rained. My phone buzzed with flood warnings and with texts from friends in Katy and Bellaire who were simply wanting to share their own amazement at the amount of water falling from the sky. I reminded myself that this neighborhood saw no flooding during Allison, that our house was above the floodplain that had been reestablished by Allison, and that I simply needed to endure Harvey's onslaught. This too shall pass.

Against the Storm

In the midst of the alarms and humming texts
that night, the Astros surrendered a 6-1 lead in the
seventh and eighth innings to lose to the Angels 7-6.
The once un-hittable bullpen was continuing its
miserable month. The August storm was upon us
both in full force now. It was time to hunker down.
Yet, as I went to bed, the battle between hope and
doubt raged openly in my mind as I lay sleeplessly.
The gentle rains that soothed my slumber the night
before were now heavy iron boot taps marching at
an attacker's pace. It was safe and quiet in Dallas, I
thought. But even in shelter, there was
sleeplessness. Judging by her text messages
passing along information and checking our status,
Dedra slept as little as I did.

Alex had blocked out the tumult of the world
around him to immerse himself in the tumult on the
screen in front of him, where he ran and jumped
over obstacles all while firing various weaponry in
the direction of his enemy. He didn't look to be on
the verge of sleep despite the advancing hour. He
was connected with his friends and passed along
reconnaissance that one of them who lived in our
former neighborhood had water in their driveway. It
was advancing on his friend's sister's car parked on
the lower part of the drive. This was a valuable
comparable data to my recollections from Allison,
and meant that Chigger Creek was likely just as high
as it was during Allison. Since Allison, there was a
new neighborhood constructed on the other side of
Chigger Creek from our old home that took away
some of the overspill area and forced a narrower

draining of the creek through that point of Friendswood. The spillage from Harvey was now leaking to our older neighborhood.

This same pattern was playing out across nearly every suburb in Houston. The freeways of the city had become impassible, many becoming channels for the vast floodwaters amassed by Harvey's relentlessly pounding rains. Thousands were stranded as flood waters isolated them in their homes, in their cars, or at their fight-night party. We were fortunate to have stayed in Friendswood. We would not have made it back. Many were stranded in the dark, trying to get from one location to another while the waters rose around them.

That night brought fear to the city, to the suburbs, to our house. Harvey showed no mercy. Nature cannot detect our fear. It cannot detect our submission. Nature is oblivious to these human conditions.

The rain comes when it comes.

And it had come. Buzzes, alarms, cracks of thunder, and the marching boots of Harvey's rains created a dark symphony of doleful melodies in my head. The night passed slowly, and I yielded to Morpheus' command only as the rains slackened before dawn.

I awoke in a quiet moment. The TV was off, my phone was quiet, and the marching of Harvey's forces had ceased for the moment. I was urged by another of nature's unstoppable forces to take certain measures before beginning my day. Though I hesitate to reconstruct them here, given their base nature, I dare not exclude them, for the next moments were a most fitting opening act to the day's theater.

Upon the completion of my commitment to digestive cycle maintenance, I took customary measures to ensure hygienic disposal. As I stepped away toward the sink, the bowl began to fill up with no suggestive sign of the normal spiraling into the pipes. I scrambled frantically, adrenaline surging me from my lazy morning state, and crouched down beneath the commode to turn the water off valve at the wall, with the contents of the bowl rising at my ear level as I twisted the knob. I worked it to the right feverishly, as if I were James Bond deactivating the mad villain's nuclear bomb. Having avoided detonation by fractions of an inch, I reached for the plunger, when it began to occur to me.

"*Uh oh.*" This wasn't a clog. "*Uh oh,*" I scrambled to the window. The backyard was covered in water, the blue of the pool water raised just above the brown flood water by virtue of its higher grade. "*Uh oh,*" I ran to the front door and opened it up.

"*Holy sh..!*"

The house was entirely surrounded by water. The streets and yards and the dividing esplanades between them were all united under Clear Creek's encroaching waters swollen by Harvey's rains. The Honda Pilot sat in the front driveway with water half way up the wheel walls. And the pathway to the door once danced upon by Harvey's ambassadors

Greg Etzel

delivering the wine was now under dominion of the flood. I stood at the threshold, three steps above the grade of the front porch. I looked out in amazement. "Houston, we have a problem."

VI. Harvey's Invasion

Harvey's forces had besieged us in the night, and a dark line in the southern sky was the leading edge of his morning assault. We would be breached. I drew upon my grandfather's inspiration, as I had all week, and focused on addressing the problem in front of me. When the Apollo 13 crew lost life support capacity in the main cabin, the crew had to seek shelter in the Lunar Module. My grandfather's team was called upon to design a carbon dioxide filtration system that could support three passengers rather than the two for which the LM was designed. To construct this device they were only able to use what the astronauts had available to them in the ship, and they had to take into account the very limited power available to them. Oh, and by the way, the clock was ticking. You've probably seen the movie. I imagined my own response to the rising floodwaters in terms of this, Houston's most famous mission, playing the role of mission control and crew.

Our situation called for an orderly withdrawal. We would need to move our operations upstairs. I opened the door to the garage and saw floodwaters seeping under the large door, crawling along the garage floor in pulsing lunges. I grabbed a Sharpie from the supply stash–I knew it would come in handy–and I marked a line on the floor. I glanced at my watch and wrote the time–9:21AM. I walked briskly upstairs to wake Alex.

Greg Etzel

"Get up! Time to get to work!"

"What!? Stop! No! Go away!" he was not welcoming of my strategic arrival.

"We've got to move stuff upstairs. The water is rising!" The urgency in my tone let him know I wasn't kidding.

"Seriously?" he shifted in bed and got to his feet.

"Important documents. Pictures. Emergency food supplies. We need to move it all upstairs." I went back downstairs as he got dressed, passing by the garage again. The water had creeped nearly half way across the floor. I glanced at my watch: 9:27 AM. It was creeping in fast! And Harvey's boot steps were growing louder outside.

Alex made his way to his window. "Holy shit!" I could hear it from downstairs.

"*Language*," I responded, as loudly, and in a tone mimicking that of a prudish Captain America in an action sequence from one of those Avengers movies we'd watched together on many a Friday family movie night. It was meant to be humorous, and perhaps inspiring. Maybe it would help Alex draw upon some imaginary superhero reference to gear himself up for our little situation, as I had been drawing upon the Apollo 13 mission for my own inspiration. Any good plan needs inspiration, imagination, and a dash of wit to succeed.

I began packing the refrigerated items that we would need/want for the next few days into an ice chest and adding dry ice to keep them cold. I left our

70

cow in the freezer knowing that it would last longer inside, sealed by the insulated door, than in any ice chest I had available to me. We carted the food upstairs, with Alex stubbornly using his recovering wrist more than I wanted him to. The adequacy of our water supplies was confirmed by the weakness in my legs from the repetitive trips upstairs.

Sharpie at the ready, I passed the garage with each trip upstairs. The water's advance came at an alarmingly increasing pace. The entire garage floor, or sub-floor as may be the case, was covered in a thin layer of water. It now had but to climb the three- or four-inch step up to the flooring that matches the grade of our downstairs living area and it would be at the threshold. Harvey's troops were climbing the walls!

"Dad, look!" Alex called to me as he looked into the back yard. "You know it's not good when the flood hits the pool level." He recognized the rising waters in our back yard encroaching now on the pool. In the heavier rains of the morning, the drops began to splash the murky brown of Harvey into the haven of blue water sitting in our backyard. Slowly, at the edges, the brown silty mess began leaking in spiral arrays into the blue until the pool was overrun with flood water. Now, in combined force, it lurched its way up the yard toward the back doors.

Maggie was very nervous and, now, just like us, without a working bathroom. We situated her upstairs in Alex's bedroom on the tile floor with her bed and food and water. We would take care of messes as they came about. Our functional needs would be addressed with slightly more decorum, but without the luxury of functioning plumbing.

At this point, I should self-disclose some deficiencies in storage practices at our household. I was discovering, as we went through this emergency relocation exercise, that we stored nearly every important document in our lives within two feet of our downstairs floor. Passports, birth certificates, insurance documents, you name it. All at floor level. Under the bed. In the closet. Always on the damned floor. The act of moving all of it upstairs gave me substantial regret that I had not audited my storage practices sooner. I attended to those crucial documents while Alex collected the stash of children's pictures, also stored in the lowest cabinets in the study.

"Dad," he called out to me as I passed by. "Is this Zach?" he asked holding up an old baby photo.

"You're not supposed to be *looking* at the photos. You're supposed to be *moving* them upstairs!" I chided him, admonishing him to get back on task. I glanced at the picture as I walked by with a box in hand. "But, yes, that's Zach as a baby."

"Ha! He was fat!" he chuckled.

"He was a baby, for crying out loud. You weren't exactly a Slim Jim yourself at that age, you know." It didn't matter; it was ammunition he would use in their sibling taunting later. "Just get back to work. We don't have much time."

The water in the garage was now

measurable. Half an inch at 10:12 AM. We needed to keep moving. The water approached the back door entering our living room. Harvey's breach of our walls was imminent.

My urgings gave stir to Alex's desire to meet Harvey head on. He gathered duct tape from the supply area, and began to seal the back door in an attempt to hold Harvey's advance, or at least gain us a little time.

"Not a bad idea," I acknowledged his youthful exuberance. "But, I'd prefer you seal off the hall bathroom. I actually more afraid of what may come out of there." The all-day chili was a tactical error.

With Alex working on the duct tape sealing procedure, I decided to pick up his original task of packing and moving the family pictures. As fate would have it, Dedra was in the midst of a photo organization process, separating photos roughly by era. It appeared to be a project about three quarters complete, enough to reach a conclusion that we have vastly more pictures of Zach, our first born, than any other child, but with ample stacks of pictures still needing assignment to the appropriate era. In fairness, most of the pictures of the twins are electronically stored, but Alex seemed underrepresented. Ammunition for his unfair middle-child treatment allegations, I suppose.

One of his photos was sitting atop a pile that was ready for sorting – and through which Alex was looking previously. He was about three or four years old in the photo, an age during which there was a

73

period of about six months where he refused to wear any shoes other than his cowboy boots. For any outfit, it didn't matter what he was wearing, the footwear was always the same pair of cowboy boots. They were beat up, scarred, and stained by an assortment of fruit juices, but they would not be parted with, even for a brand-new pair of boots. When we ultimately threw the boots in the trash to force the issue, the boot-wearing phase passed. In the photo, he had those old boots on with a pair of overly short shorts and some generic plaid tee-shirt. He looked ridiculously Texan.

I chuckled and recalled a time during this "boot phase" when some older kids in the local park were teasing him over the fact that he was wearing them to play at the playground. It didn't faze Alex a bit. Later, one of the older kids began shaking a bridge connecting two parts of the playground equipment upon which Alex was walking in an effort to disrupt Alex's balance. Alex grabbed the rails with both hands, steadying himself, raised his head slowly and stared the much bigger kid squarely in the eye and declared, "You better stop that, now." He didn't yell. He delivered the message softly, but with a sternness in his eye that ignored the obvious size advantage his opponent possessed and gave the impression that at least Alex believed he was capable of making the kid stop. Whether he was right or wrong in that belief would never be known, as the older kid decided the matter wasn't worthy of his attention and went about doing other things.

Alex's initiation of the duct tape procedure was a relic of the inner-tenacity he showed as a little boot-wearing toddler. He was a good guy to have around in this fight. Unfortunately, I seemed to have his same knack for picking out opponents.

I continued to flip through several more photos before hearing, "Dad....Dad!"

His calling broke me from my distraction. I had been lured by the Sirens' song of sweet memories of years gone by. They soothed my anxious mind, yet in their comfort I had become derelict in my duties. "The water! It's coming in!" he was pointing to the garage door that opened into the kitchen area. Harvey's troops had scaled the step separating the two grades and were leaking over the threshold and under the door. "You can look at pictures later!" he declared, without the sarcastic tones I would have expected given that I was caught in a moment of parental hypocrisy. He was fully engaged in the flood defense strategy, and perhaps himself aware of the pull of Sirens' sweet voices.

His calls sprang me back into action. With Homeric appreciation, I flung the loose pictures into the boxes, took my leave of the memories, and carried the boxes upstairs. His duct tape procedure had bought time at the back door, but the water was seeping through the tape. Harvey would not be held back by adhesive. We hurried our pace, but so did Harvey, slamming us with another phalanx of heavy rains. We made a few final runs with water sloshing at our heels before succumbing to fatigue.

Greg Etzel

"We got what we could," I told Alex in a voice
meant to convey my appreciation for his efforts.
"Drink a bottle of water," I pushed a bottle from our
emergency stash in front of him. "Hydrate or die," I
said, echoing our favorite hiking tip from my good
friend, Cyril, with whose family we had hiked up a
mountain ridge in Colorado a few years back.
"Hydrate or die" was his go to statement when he
went to his water bottle for a drink, and he would
encourage us to do the same. He was very smart,
very straightforward, and succinct just like the advice
he conveyed. "Hydrate or die," his words came again
from my mouth as I drank my own bottle.

"Do you think they'll cancel school
tomorrow?" Alex turned to me and asked with a wry
grin. Despite the conditions, his humor remained dry.
In it I saw my father–his dry humor the tool for
diffusing any overly intense situation growing up.

"It's starting to look like a distinct possibility," I
replied with emphasized understatement.

As we relaxed for the moment I checked my
phone and found several messages from family and
friends from across the country wanting to know our
status. Harvey had made the national spotlight. We
had been too absorbed with our own operations to
check in on the world outside our doors. We turned
on the local news and saw Friendswood streets and
homes underwater. People were wading out of their
neighborhoods in chest deep high water. Boats were
beginning to launch into streets to find people
trapped in their homes. And the news footage was

only a mile or so upstream on Clear Creek from us. Our morning's struggles against Harvey became trivial by comparison, but served as a reminder of the very real dangers we were now facing. It was not time to panic, however. It was time to plan.

We had successfully secured ourselves upstairs with provisions to sustain us for several days. The water would still need to rise 8-10 feet before it would reach us upstairs. I convinced myself that we were a little farther from the banks of the creek than the upstream neighborhood featured on the news. But the entire neighborhood up there was underwater, and the rain was not stopping, although it had relented over the last hour. I kept a mark on the wall downstairs with the sharpie every half hour to determine the rate of increase. It appeared to be climbing at around an inch and a half per hour, which would give us plenty of time to plan for the emergency exit procedure, should it become necessary.

Our neighborhood area was generally flat like the rest of Houston, so just being able to float and paddle should get us to higher ground, the local HEB grocery store likely being the highest spot around, only a mile or so away. We sloshed into the garage and grabbed the surfboard and some child-sized life jackets we still had from several years ago. If it came to it, we'd leave through the upstairs windows and float until we could walk.

Emergency exit procedure determined, I checked in with Dedra, who'd been calling to check on us. I ensured her that we were fine, that water was in the house, but it that had a long way to go before it got to us. I mentioned that we were making preparations in case the waters continued to rise.

"Take the ax with you if you go in the attic," she said as she was playing out scenarios in her head that she had heard from the news. "Someone died because they were trapped in the attic by the flood waters and they had no way out."

"I think we will jettison and take our chances getting to dry land before we get in the attic," I said. Regardless, I assured her I would bring the hatchet upstairs along with the other emergency items we were gathering, but I didn't expect we would be using it.

"And the air mattress. Blow up the air mattress. I saw someone floating out of their neighborhood on an air mattress." She'd been watching news coverage all morning, and it had inflamed her worries. She was eager to communicate any survival tip she had learned from the thousands upon thousands of people facing perils much graver than our own. We learned from her that Harvey had claimed the lives of local victims, one here in Friendswood. Alex's former driving instructor had perished in the rising flood waters of Coward's Creek not too far away from us. Everything on the screen and in her report brought testimony of Harvey's capricious destruction, and it was all very, very close to home.

I responded to other messages and went

back down to mark the water's climb. It was creeping up the wall, four inches or so from the ground, and the timing calculations based on my markings suggested a stable rise of an inch or so an hour. The rain had lightened considerably in the middle of the day, but the water continued to rise.

In the midst of my wall-marking procedure, the doorbell rang. It was my neighbor, Jack, dressed in chest high waders.

"You guys doing ok?" he inquired.

"Yeah, the water got in, but we've moved operations upstairs," I stood to greet him on the only dry portion of our downstairs, the small raised entryway that meets the steps up to the house.

"You've still got power, too, I see," he replied. "Whole street seems to still have it. Water is at our porch but not in yet. I shut off our AC though because it was under water." It was actually quite remarkable that we still had power and air conditioning despite the tempest that had swirled around us. His house was two houses up the street from ours, and a little bit further from the creek.

"I probably should shut mine off as well. The fan units are raised but not high enough for this much water," I replied. "That's a good suit to have around today!" I commented on his waders. The irony was not lost on me that my preparations did not adequately take into account a proper suit for traversing the floodwaters! My grandfather and uncle spent their entire careers developing and perfecting suits so that humans could withstand the dangers of space, and I gave no prior consideration to my flood attire.

"I've got an extra pair in my garage, if you want to use 'em. They're kind of hot, though. Neoprene and built for winter duck hunts." His offer was graciously accepted, whether or not he recognized the internal shame I was feeling at my sartorial oversight. I followed him through the just below chest deep waters in the street between our houses. I tried not to think of the Protozoan army swirling around me. I would be glad to have the suit.

Suit in hand, a procedure was developed for conducting extra-shelter activities, or *EVAs* as I was referring them in homage to the NASA term for fully suited activities outside of a spacecraft (i.e., "extra-vehicular activities"). I instructed Alex that that before entering flood water areas the suit would be donned at the base of the staircase by the front door in the entryway, which remained several inches above the floodwaters in the house. After an EVA was completed, the suit would be removed and hung over the bannister until the next mission.

"Will you stop calling it that, please?" Alex interrupted the training session.

"What? EVA?"

"Yes. That's so nerdy, even for you. Stop."

"Oh, come on, it makes it sound so much cooler –'I'm embarking on an EVA to monitor the air circulation life support systems' just sounds way better than 'I'm going outside to check the AC.'" I tried to convince him to go along with me. He would have ten years ago.

"No. No, it does not sound cooler. That, I can assure you."

"Fine, then. *I'm going to walk around outside and check the AC unit.* I will be back." I reluctantly abandoned my theme, and emphasized my abandonment facetiously in my response.

"I want to try out the suit when you get back from walking around," he said, retreating upstairs.

"Back from my *EVA*, you mean," I mumbled softly, donning the suit and stepping into the five or so inches of floodwater now circulating in the living room.

VII. Still Raining

My initial suited EVA took me into the back yard from the patio by way of the French doors that connect the outside patio to our living room/kitchen table area. With each step on the lawn, the ground gave way like a soft sponge. The water was up to my thighs as I made my way to the back of the house to monitor the air circulation life support systems, or the air conditioning units, as Alex would prefer that I call them. Harvey had unleashed other insidious forces with his rains. Beyond the more dangerous and unseen single-celled creatures, less dangerous but more visually frightening creatures lurked about in disturbingly large numbers. Spiders skirted across the surface of the water, little brown water beetles swam, and islands of red hell floated about me as I waded cautiously in my unrecognizable back yard. I gave widest berth to the fire ants.

Most Texans are familiar with the natural defense mechanism that fire ant colonies have developed for surviving floodwaters, well, most of them anyway. Entire colonies ball up together tightly and float along the surface of the water until they can attach to something that will allow them to crawl onto dry ground. The ants on the bottom die, drowning in a sacrificial act for the greater good of the colony. It is a noble demonstration that would otherwise invoke my empathy, if not for the fact that they are fire ants. I've been bitten by a handful of fire ants in the past, and can only imagine the pain that a football-sized mound of them would inflict. So, I walked at a respectful distance from the large ant ball that was floating between the pool and the hedges. But mostly, I kept watch for snakes—water moccasins in particular—coming up from the creek. That was my greatest fear.

I've come across a few snakes jogging in the wooded trails in Friendswood, and I have found that most begin to slither away once they feel the heavy plods of my footsteps on the ground or see my large silhouette lumbering forward toward them. But I have noticed that one species, the water moccasin, does not yield its ground for humans in the same manner other snakes do. I once came upon a water moccasin laying on the pavement of the parking lot under my car door when I returned from a jog. I approached the car from a distance, loudly stomping my feet as I marched closer, but the snake just lay there unperturbed. I opened the back door of the FJ and pulled out an old golf club and began to bang the ground around it, in the hopes of *scaring it off with a stick,* but as I got close to it, the moccasin coiled its body and assumed an attack posture in a manner suggesting it was ready to defend its current position beneath my door. I felt very much like how the bigger kid on the playscape bridge staring down *little cowboy-boot Alex* must have felt. Surely, I could just crush this snake with my superior size and tools, but that was not really the right thing to do. This was as much his park as mine, and it was quite possible he could get off a hell of a bite. I decided to crawl through from the passenger side, happy with the compromise.

In that encounter, I was nervous on solid pavement. Running into a water moccasin in thigh high water on soaked turf didn't exactly give me comforting thoughts. Fortunately, I saw no snakes, but the water level was definitely going to create AC problems. I returned inside to shut them down, much to my dread. August in Houston without air conditioning, even with the rain-cooled skies, was miserable. We would be sweating from this point forward, though the electricity was still working so we could at least run the fans upstairs. Despite this momentary optimism, electricity would be our next concern.

Soon the water would rise to the point where it would pour into the outlets on the wall. Mind you, I have no electrical training whatsoever, despite having installed a few ceiling fans and light fixtures in my day. But my thought, based on my limited understanding of the working of electrical currents, was that water flowing into powered outlets would likely not be a good thing. Receiving responses from friends and the world wide web varying from, "it should be fine, they will shut off automatically" to "there's a chance your home could be engulfed in flames while you sleep," I decided to err on the side of caution and develop a procedure for shutting the power down manually.

The breaker box is outside on the back wall behind our bedroom, which is along a wall that runs from the back porch area around a corner and to an area, guarded by shoulder tall hedges, that holds the AC units and electrical breakers for all areas of the house. When the time came, an EVA would be conducted to flip the switches on the breaker box manually. Special precautions would be taken on the EVA, and during the switch-flipping process, that were designed to ensure the safety of the crewmember conducting the procedure. In addition to the standard rubberized suit required for any EVA, rubber kitchen gloves would be worn on both hands. A step ladder and a wooden baseball bat would be carried to the breaker boxes as part of the EVA. The stepladder would be deployed and then used by the crewmember to stand above the water as he shut down the power, in the unlikely event there was some type of arc of electricity created by the flipping of the switch. The bat was primarily for snakes, but could be used to flip the switches as an additional item between the rubber gloves and the breaker switches.

I gathered the necessary materials for conducting the power-down procedure and placed them on a table I had moved into the entry-way, which served as our decontamination chamber between the flooded downstairs beneath it, and the shelter upstairs. Procedure developed, I decided to wait until the water got closer to the outlets before conducting it. There was no sense in shutting it down too soon, as power was so vital to our communications and electronic distractions. By my estimate, we still had a couple hours before it had to be initiated, but we were ready with a plan. Identify a problem. Assess the situation. Develop a procedure for solving it. Modify as necessary. That was the approach. Every procedure an act of defiance against Harvey, every plan a tool to wrest control from the grasp of the storm.

With the rains still light, I decided to continue my walk around in the new EVA suit. The pool was virtually invisible, its overrun long complete. The FJ Cruiser, which I now began to refer to in my head as the Lunar Module or *Lem* (as NASA folks pronounce its abbreviation), sat outside the garage driveway with water nearly over the tires. It appeared that the engine block was above the water line, but it was close. Water was not yet inside the doors, although its rubber floors would hardly be fazed by it. As I walked around the house, I saw that Harvey's waters had surrounded us entirely. The streets were impassible, above waist deep in the center. I chatted with some of my neighbors who had also stayed behind to face the storm. They seemed to be faring a little better than us, at least with respect to the amount of water in their houses, but they all suggested that they had no more room to give before inundation.

As I walked down the street in the direction of the creek, the sounds of a helicopter hummed in the distance. The rhythmic sound of the rotors grew louder as I walked, and soon a military-style transport helicopter appeared low overhead, flying south not too far above the tree line. Someone huddled in white towels sat in the side door area along with the rescue personnel. They flew by with a fading buzz in one direction only to be replaced by the sound of more rotors coming from the same direction from which the first helicopter had just come. As I got closer to the end of the street, I began to feel the pull of the creek's current. Fire ant colonies were migrating south toward League City on its flow, and I dodged balls of various sizes. The house at the end of our street was built up high above the grade of the street at the back of our neighborhood. A park behind it abuts Clear Creek. The house was an island to itself, and the park was now simply part of Clear Creek, the current of the floodwaters flowing visibly stronger through it. Harvey asserted dominion over the back half of our neighborhood and was now pillaging the houses, from lowest to highest.

I returned to our house and inspected the downstairs, primarily to see where the water was the closest to the electrical outlets. In the course of my inspection, I found that a number of items, previously deemed by members of our family to be lost, were in fact, not lost. Largest in number of these items were hair bands. I cannot begin to count the number of hours I've spent searching for a hairband when trying to help Grace get ready for soccer practice or school. They are never anywhere to be found, no matter how hard I search. But as I walked around now, they greeted me at every turn, floating atop the surface of the six inches of water that was circulating in lazy patterns in the downstairs. The flood also dislodged all those hidden individual socks from their mysterious hiding places. Like the hairbands, these mate-less socks littered the flood-scape and highlighted to the mess that it was.

I ended my EVA and passed the suit to Alex for his turn. When he returned, we passed the afternoon and early evening watching the news and trading texts with friends and family who were experiencing all of this with us. I worked my way back to the supply stash.

"Hey, are you hungry? I think it's chow time," I proclaimed. I cracked open a can of bean dip, a jar of salsa and opened a bag of chips. A fully balanced meal was ready.

"Bean dip? Nasty. Who eats bean dip?" Alex said, somewhat disappointed it seemed with the menu selection.

"What do you mean who eats bean dip? Everybody, that's who," I responded with no small dose of incredulity. "It's like the perfect emergency supply food. Protein, fat, and the chips for simple carbohydrates."

"I think you've got plenty of reserve," he teased.

"Ha ha. You're very funny. Well, I don't think Whataburger is open, so you're stuck with it."

We sat at the bar table in the back of the TV room upstairs, watching it in amazement. It was a surreal combination of rescue scenes and weather reports, with reporters making valiant, if not always successful, efforts to remain calm in the midst of the unfolding chaos. We heard reports of rescues like those going on up the creek from us in Friendswood happening all over the Houston area. Freeways were impassible; surface streets were no better. People were fleeing their homes with whatever belongings they could grab and trying to find shelter. Harvey had dealt the city a massive and widespread blow. The weather reporters continued to awe at the amount of rain that Harvey had produced in the last 24 hours. Worse still, they could offer no comfort that it would stop.

The rain comes when it comes.

It was quiet outside our now-open windows, with only a gentle rain. But in other areas, the rain continued to fall hard. My friend Tom, who lived in Katy, was sending updates that involved copious amounts of rain. The great Katy prairie that once served as a natural reservoir for the Houston area, was now home to a million people and their homes and businesses, including Tom. Harvey seemed set to retake nature's domain. The Addicks and Barker Reservoirs, which served to preserve some of the valuable Katy prairie and hold back water from the Buffalo Bayou watershed that flows through the heart of Houston, were full. Indeed, all around the city, reservoirs were pushed to their utmost limits. Creeks and bayous swelled into homes and roads. And people fled in masses. Friendswood was not the only area hit hard by unheard of rains, Clear Creek not the only waterway to reach record heights, nor was it the only town to lose a citizen to the havoc wrought by Harvey. The news relayed reports that a police officer had been killed in the floodwater while attempting to get to a rescue. People were clinging to the tops of their cars, to trees, to whatever they could grab. It was a perilous day.

But in the midst of it all, everyday Houstonians stepped out from the safety of their dry ground to use their personal assets to rescue complete strangers. Houstonians who owned boats or very large trucks—and if you're familiar with Houston, you know that to be a sizable portion the population—began arriving to conduct missions into the waters to bring people to dry ground. We watched the scenes in awe, and not a little pride.

"It's sort of like that movie *Dunkirk* we saw this summer," Alex commented on a news scene showing many little John-boats, air boats, canoes, pool toys, all being used to ferry people to shelter.

"It really is," I had to concur with the observation. It was indeed similar. Harvey hit us all with an onslaught of water we'd not seen before, a natural *blitzkrieg.* Houstonians were staggered by the blow and trapped by the rising waters of Harvey's continued advance. And there were not enough troops to manage a defense. But neighbors reached out to neighbors and, in the midst of the rains, flotillas of civilian rescue boats of all shapes and sizes sprang into action to save further casualties. It was a truly remarkable and historic scene unfolding in the streets of Houston, and I cheered on the unknown heroes who got off of their couches and into their canoes in defiance of Harvey.

"We will never surrender. Never ever surrender," I started speaking in my best Winston Churchill voice.

"Stop. Just, just stop." Alex did not appreciate my impersonation as much as I did. Perhaps he began to recognize, as I now had, the surreal events unfolding around us. Our home, our city, we ourselves were being tested by forces not before seen. Harvey felt like something much more than a storm. Alex knew my Churchill voice was designed to capture that gravity.

"Do you think they will cancel school tomorrow?" he asked with a grin.

As day gave way to night, it did so with relative calm, if only in our house in Friendswood. The waters downstairs had not increased above the six-to-seven inch mark and had begun to slowly retreat in the evening with the lighter rains of the day. At this rate, it appeared that we may have power through the night. We used our power to continue communicating with our friends and family around the city and state. Dedra was relaxed by the relative calm of our afternoon and my assurances that the water had begun to recede in the lighter rains of the day. My friends in Katy and Bellaire texted with periodic reports indicating that our lighter rains were not shared universally. They endured the heaviest rounds of rain all day.

On the weather map, Harvey was making erratic and unusual movements back toward the coastline, as if he was returning to the sea for more ammunition. His slow wanderings throughout the day had spared Friendswood direct blows from the heavy bands of rain that hammered us the previous night and morning, though it never quite stopped raining. The troublesome bands had been concentrated to the west of us, where my friends Tom, John, and Kevin were texting concerns about the water rising toward their houses. Though his moves were erratic, it was nevertheless clear that Harvey was slowly creeping in our direction.

We shared another meal that night—a meat and cheese plate with sandwich meats and cheese slices, served with crackers or bread, and a side of salsa to ensure proper vegetable intake. For a musical accompaniment, I queued up a little Credence Clearwater Revival on my phone— *Who'll Stop the Rain* with random selections to follow. It seemed fitting for the occasion. We enjoyed the meal in the muggy night air, the loss of AC being made tolerable by the fan's circulating the moist air about us. It was bearable and made more so by the recognition of our relative comfort compared to those on the TV screen in front of us. Dramas played out seemingly on the half-hour, with an ever-increasing sense of despair. Alex abandoned the real drama to reconnect with his friends, while I stayed parked on the couch.

Near midnight, the Army Corps of Engineers was forced to make a decision to open one of the Katy reservoirs, an act that would flood hundreds of people's homes in Katy in an effort to save thousands more homes in Houston from the imminent failure of the massive levy itself. The officer advised that the waters would begin to flood the homes in several neighborhoods (my friend Tom's thankfully not among them) late in the morning tomorrow. The people living in those neighborhoods were urged to evacuate. But evacuate to where? How would they get out? Virtually all of the roads in the area were impassable. Traffic reporters studied maps with flashing markers all over them, trying to discern routes covering terrain that was not underwater. But the options were few. The soon-to-be evacuees had nowhere safe to go.

In the midnight darkness, a general anxiety permeated the TV screen and found its way into our upstairs shelter. It had been clear for some time that no one had seen anything like Harvey before. From the new colors on the rainfall maps to the traffic maps that flashed with road closure symbols at every route, an overall sense pervaded, even from the most seasoned professionals, that we were in the middle of an event beyond all prior experience.

The battle between hope and doubt raged on in my restless sleep, as it did with every Houstonian that night. Our orderly withdrawal upstairs had been a success, and we had been the beneficiaries of lighter rain. We had reason for optimism. But as we drifted off to sleep in the early morning hours, Harvey was conducting his maneuvers and readying himself for his next assault. We had enjoyed a brief respite. But our battle was not over.

VIII. The Hammer & Anvil

A strange calm enveloped the room the next morning when I awoke on the couch. The TV was still on, beaming a morning traffic report that can be adequately summarized as: "Stay home. All the roads are closed." I walked downstairs to find only puddles of water remaining on the floor, the floodwaters having retreated in the night all the way out to the middle of the yard. My spirits were lifted measurably, despite the filthy mess that was left behind.

Given the substantial drainage, I decided to run a flush test procedure on an empty toilet to see if the plumbing was operational. It was a successful procedure. Immediately, the downstairs hall bathroom was unsealed and a flush procedure executed. Flood waters had penetrated the attempted duct tape seal, but the waters did not reach a level that would have resulted in Chernobyl-esque consequences. The morning's respite gave an opportunity to eliminate the enemy from within that had lurked during yesterday's battles, perched precariously above the diffusing and commingling powers of the floodwaters. The opportunity was seized with successful results, and spirits were further lifted.

It was easy to get lulled into sense of finality with the way the morning's events were unfolding. The withdrawal of the flood water from its position in

94

the house boosted my morale as if I were witnessing the retreat of Harvey's invading army. Nasty little reminders of his presence remained littered about, an uncomfortable number of bugs, mostly spiders and water beetles, scavenged about in the newly drying living room floor. I eliminated the scavenging marauders with well-timed stomps where I could.

"We're going to need to call the exterminator," I muttered to myself. I knew that lurking in the dark crevices and in the water-soaked walls were the most feared, albeit harmless, creatures of the insect world—the Texas tree roach. Memories of Hurricane Alicia sprang fresh to my mind. I knew they would scurry in on the water's edge and seek shelter in areas from which they had been banned by various chemical means that had now been diluted or eliminated by the floodwaters. Harvey unlocked that chemical barrier, and urged their incursion on his rising flow. I stood aware and ready to face them. Unlike the one that haunted my family in 1983, these invaders would not escape. I conducted the morning EVA with a confidence in my stride.

Moments later, though, during breakfast at the central command table upstairs, news reports gave rise to concern. Harvey was on the move in our direction. His odd wanderings to the south toward the Gulf of Mexico on the previous day had repositioned the storm to now take a new line of attack on the city of Houston. Worse still, this time the attack would come with the tidal surge of a tropical storm. While the surge would not be significant in size compared to the initial direct assault on Rockport a few days ago, it would act as a force against any waters attempting to drain into Galveston Bay. This essentially affected every single drainage channel in the Houston area. We weren't watching a retreat; this was a flanking maneuver!

It was a classic *hammer and anvil* tactic that Alexander the Great himself would have admired. Harvey would array his forces from the sea, depleted though they may be, along the Galveston Bay escape route, hampering any waters attempting to drain from the Houston area, while simultaneously launching a *hammer* attack with new bands of rain that were forming in columns now marching in from off the coast. Alexander used the precise same approach with his phalanx and cavalry units to conquer armies from Persia to Africa to India in 334-326 BC. Indeed, I began to think that Harvey's attack came with a subtle wink aimed directly for me.

My son Alex, or Alexander Charles, bears his name in honor of Alexander the Great and his maternal grandfather and my own maternal grandfather, who had been my inspiration all week—Charles. It was our family naming convention; each child's first name was a name we liked but was unique (at least in our family) to that child, and the middle name was given to honor a family member. His middle name, Charles, worked as a two for one. At the time Alex was born, the name *Alexander* was one Dedra and I both liked, though I admit my admiration originated because I had been watching some show on the History Channel, that turned into a book, and then a board game recreating some of Alexander's epic battlefield victories. It was a brief Alexander the Great fascination phase, but perfectly timed, to contribute to the naming of my second son who now fought by my side. Harvey's maneuvers seemed remarkably coincidental, as if designed to convey a knowledge of my inner-workings and to use them to taunt me.

It was a reminder that I had more to battle than the winds and the rain. I had dared to look upon the sun, to gaze at its shiny crown as it glistened around the edge of darkness itself. I had stared into the abyss. This challenge began before Harvey was formed. I invoked internal storms of faith and doubt, of hope and despair. My battle with Harvey was about more than staying dry. Every plan I made, every procedure I conducted, was an act of defiance against the forces of despair that Harvey had unleashed with his thunderous rains.

"Bring it on!" I thought. I would not relent to the darker forces brought upon me by Harvey's design. We will stand our ground between hammer and anvil, and we will survive.

Our fighting spirit was but a fraction of that displayed on the continuously streaming news. The rescuers, both professional first responders and average citizens with boats, continued to pull people from treacherous situations and take them to shelter. It was a remarkable display of the spirit of the city, worthy of the *Dunkirk* comparison Alex had made. Houston has a long history of defying the forces of nature, and not simply by virtue of its experience with tropical storms–for there was no such comparable storm to Harvey.

Houston had the spirit to put a man on the moon, turning science fiction into historical fact. Houston pioneered the transplanting of artificial hearts and other heart-saving surgeries, developed innovative treatments for cancers, and created vaccines and therapies that delay the very agents of death itself. Houstonians do not back down from the challenges of nature. They arise, roll up their sleeves, and fight like hell. That is exactly what Alex and I saw when we watched the news streaming on TV. The unnamed heroes in the streets inspired us to continue our fight and gave us an awareness of our relative position in this unfolding disaster.

Dedra checked in on our status. I explained our situation and the flanking maneuver Harvey made in the night. I told her that I expected the water to make its way back in the house when Harvey hit us again. That really wasn't a concern. After all, once six inches of your downstairs is destroyed by flood, it really doesn't matter if it floods again, at least until a certain point. I considered the risk that the water could rise to the level of the upstairs to be remote. But we were prepared for it.

"You've got the hatchet, right?" she inquired, not wanting us to be trapped in the attic and drowned by rising waters as one person had.

"I told you already, we are not getting in the attic. We will bail long before we need to go into the attic," I reminded her. I had absolutely no desire to climb into the dark, enclosed attic with its unfinished floor and scores of metal parts and wires from the various air conditioning and water heating elements of the house. "We'll take our chances getting up the street to higher ground. Maggie can float on the air mattress. Alex and I will take the life vests and surfboard as floatation. I don't think we will have to swim very far. Just up the street to the front of the neighborhood." I hadn't given thought to the actual timing of that decision, but it was something I needed to address.

"I'm not sure when we'll be able to get back to Houston. The freeways are all closed. The city is isolated. We all want to get back soon." It had been a long weekend away for them now and was turning longer.

"It has to stop raining before you can even consider that. And it has not stopped raining. In fact, it never seems to stop raining. It will settle into a nice quiet drizzle from time to time, but I don't think it ever really stops. And it's about to start raining hard again." Perhaps she heard a sort of nervous tension in my voice. We *were* caught between the hammer and the anvil. Despite my resolve, I could not pretend that I was not nervous, particularly to one who knows me so well.

"Be careful," she urged as we said goodbye and turned our attention to the skies. She was monitoring websites that reported the level of area creeks, in particular Clear Creek at the FM528 crossing. It was valuable data provided by the Harris County Flood Control District. In fact, if you were to search their database and look at the time period from the late evening of August 26, 2017, to the late morning of August 27, 2017, you will see a line that graphs the creek's rise during the first flood from four feet to nearly 16 feet. The line is nearly at a 90-degree angle. The water rose incredibly quickly. It had stabilized and even dropped somewhat during the night and morning (as evidenced by the retreat from our downstairs). Knowing the creek's level with Dedra's updates on the hour would be incredibly helpful in assessing the timing of any evacuation plan.

I also spoke to Zach, who had been following the Harvey news stories from a distance. He was beginning classes the next day far away from Houston in Memphis where normalcy still existed. In the morning, coffee shops would be buzzing, classrooms teaching, streets humming with traffic. No road or school closures. No electrical outages. Not even the need for an umbrella. Normal seemed so far removed sitting in the midst of the floodwaters. He expressed his concern and desire to back with us, facing the storm. When he was younger, he and I returned the day that Hurricane Ike left town, to find a house with no power, several downed trees and large amounts of storm debris. We spent days cutting trees and cleaning up in the hot, miserable weather that followed the storm. Nothing remotely enjoyable came out of the clean-up, but it was a sort of shared adventure—the kind that appear far fonder on reflection. I assured him that he was much better off where he was in Memphis, far from the clutches of Harvey.

Long bands of heavy thunderstorms, the ones that show up in red or purple on the fancy weather radar maps, were forming in the Gulf of Mexico and were making their spiraling march to engage the city in another assault. We were hearing the booming steps of the beginning of long line of storms. It was time to brace for the attack. We assumed our positions–Alex went to play video games, and I continued watching the news. We both kept in contact with our friends who were communicating their status.

We were battered by a line of heavy thunderstorms, and my phone buzzed with numerous alerts. While I found the flash flood warnings a bit comedic, the tornado watch alerts at least gave appreciated information. Maggie began to bark nervously again. She had settled down in Alex's room, but remained anxious throughout the storm. She wanted nothing to do with the downstairs when I tried to take her outside earlier in the day when the waters had receded. The world was too foreign to her for any comfort. She needed the security of Alex's room and her soft bed. The heaviest rain bands disrupted any of the little comfort she could find in the mad world around her.

As Harvey pounded down upon us, we

remained steadfast in our shelter. The afternoon was fading into evening and the heavy boots continued marching on outside. Despite the rain's onslaught, I felt upbeat, the city's spirit fueling my own. I decided that the dinner musical accompaniment for the evening would be something reflective of our defiant stance against all that nature was bringing to bear upon us. I opened a can of bean dip, a jar of salsa, and a bottle of Cabernet, another from Harvey's special delivery. I queued up the musical selection that I decided would be our anthem for the night on my phone, and burst in on Alex, who was playing video games in Harrison's room:

"*At first, I was afraid, I was petrified,*" I began to match Gloria Gaynor, if not in tone, then at least in timing.

"Oh God, no!" Alex responded unfavorably, perhaps more to my performance than to my selection. It was difficult to tell.

"*I kept thinking I could not go on to face your rising tide.*" I modified the lyrics slightly to better reflect our circumstances.

"Oh, please, no," his voice softening, his resolve steady.

"*But then I spent the last few nights just thinkin' how you done me wrong…*"

"For the love of God, no, don't…."

"*That I grew strong,*" I inserted a spin dance move here culminating in a bicep flex.

"You just did that…."

"'*I learned how to get along.*' Come on, sing it with me, now," I prompted him enthusiastically.

I continued without accompaniment, "*And so you're back from outer space,*

I just walked in to find you here, with that look upon your face."

"Yeah, it's the look that says, 'close the door.'"

"*I should have changed that stupid lock, I should have made you leave your key*"

"Yes, I should have. Go away."

"*If I had known for just one second you'd be back to bother me.*"

"Yes, yes, you are bothering me. Now go," he could not have accidently nailed the timing of the words *Now go* any better. I pointed in praise.

"*Walk out the door,*" I sang more enthusiastically with the gleeful acknowledgement of his accidental participation. I think I may have even caught the sign of a grin in the corner of his face. "*Just turn around now, you're not welcome anymore.*" Again, I gave the spin move in the door frame and performed a pantomime walk out the bedroom door.

"Good, now shut it behind you," Alex liked the move.

"*Cause you're not welcome anymore.*"

"No, you're not."

"*Weren't you the one who tried to hurt me with goodbye,*" Gloria and I were in synch at least.

"Yes, goodbye. Shut the door."

"*You think I'd crumble?*"

"You're not stopping are you?"

"Not before the chorus, come on, take this part home, *'You think I'd lay down and die?"* I pointed to Alex for the flourishing accompaniment.

"*Not I, I will survive. As long as I know how to love I know I'll stay alive. I've got all my life to live, and I've got all my love to give,*" I was continuing to carry the full weight of the musical performance, and to my typical reviews. All the kids seemed to go along better with sing-alongs many years ago. I really needed Grace there, she might have gone along with me. Regardless, I persisted.

He got up from his chair and came toward the door.

"*I will survive. I will survive, yeah, yeah,*" I belted out loudly; Gloria would have been so proud.

He reached out and shut the door. I felt it was a solid performance. I at least got to the chorus. I opened the door again, and in my speaking voice said to him.

"Our dinner time snack is ready."

"Let me guess. Bean dip," he said moving back to his chair.

"Only the finest. Jalapeño flavored tonight. And a new salsa I thought we'd try," I kept the door open and walked back to the central command table, picking back up with the song,"*I used to cry, but now I hold my head up high...*"

"I will come eat, if you will stop singing and turn your old man music off," Alex set forth the conditions for his partaking in the emergency-food-feast set before him.

"Ok, I will stop singing. But I will *not* turn the music off. This is a classic disco selection, perfectly tailored for our defiant stand against nature."

"It's old people music. It's like for a roller skate birthday party or something."

"You have no appreciation for great music, whatsoever. I think we may have to do an entire 70s retrospective tonight, to improve your understanding of musical literature," I threatened to continue my musical selections with further criticism.

We ate our snack and watched the weather radar on TV. We were on the front edge of a wide band of heavy rain. We could feel it coming down. The darkness of the stormy skies masked the transition from evening to nightfall. Harvey's phalanxes were charging hard, smashing us with waves of water as they had before. In the darkness, it was difficult to see the water rising, but we knew it had to be creeping closer. The hammer was hammering. I checked in on my friend Brad, who lived on the bay in Galveston. He indicated the water was beginning to rise up on his pier and lap up onto his deck. The tidal surge was pushing Galveston Bay towards his doors even as the bands of rain skirted just to his west. The anvil was in place. Brad had concerns with the high tide that was coming late in the night/early in the morning, as it would act as a boost to the strength of Harvey's holding forces.

The rainfall rates continued to impress me, to impress everyone. Sheets upon sheets of rain constantly fell from the skies. The heavy band of rain belted us for an hour, before relenting to a slower rain, which only was leading to the next band of red-radar blob working its way to us. I went downstairs to get a better view of the water level in the yard. It was already to the base of the house in front and was creeping into the garage again. I decided to suit up for an EVA to move the FJ Cruiser to a higher position.

"I am going to move the Lem, to try to keep as much of it above water as possible," I informed Alex as I prepared for the procedure.

"What's the Lem?" he inquired.

"It's short for lunar module, it was the life boat in the Apollo 13 story kind of like the FJ...."

"I told you that is very geeky, stop doing that," he interrupted me.

His remonstration had no effect. I suited up and drove the LM/FJ Cruiser from the driveway in front of the garage, where the bottom parts of its wheels were already under a couple of inches of water, through part of the back yard and up on to the patio right by the back door. The faux stone floor of the patio was at least eight to ten inches higher than the grade of the driveway, and that might make a difference in keeping the LM operative. The procedure was uneventful, though the walk outside revealed that the water was indeed on the rise.

Against the Storm

By natural law, the water made the same assault upon the house as it had before. First, into the garage it flowed, then in through the back door and garage-kitchen door, and then the back bedroom door, before rising up the walls. The water came in with a brutally efficient familiarity, as if retaking already conquered ground. That I knew the water's path of attack was of no consequence. Harvey *wanted* me to know its path. Harvey had revealed his tactics, ancient as they were, so that I would understand him. Or so I would know that he understood me. He had flooded us yesterday so we would know how he would attack us again tonight. Harvey knew what I had still yet to truly learn. It would not matter what I know.

The rain comes when it comes.

IX. The Procedure

The rain came, and it came, relentless in its assault. I had forgotten to write down the time when I checked the water coming in the garage door earlier, and I couldn't remember it now as I went back downstairs to see the water rising up the base of the wall. How long had it been? No way it had been an hour, had it? The water was now at least an inch high on the wall. This was most certainly a higher flow rate than before. I marked the wall with my Sharpie—11:48 PM. I had no idea what day of the week it was. I knew only that it was late at night on the second night after the water breached our house the first time. I kept track of time only to measure the rate of the water's rise. Otherwise, it was meaningless. There was only daytime and nighttime.

And it was certainly getting into the depths of night. Throughout the day, Dedra was giving me periodic updates of the flood level of Clear Creek when she got them. After falling all day, the water levels were rising in the night, and now were approaching 15 feet, near its high mark from the day before. The rain showed no sign of ceasing.

If possible, and I am not sure that it is, it seemed as if it came down even harder than it had two days before. Thunderous cracks broke through the sound of pounding rain as if they were the very whip of Harvey himself, urging on his minions of despair. In the darkness, I could only see the waves pouring from the eaves above the upstairs windows, as if I were looking out from a cave shrouded by a waterfall. My texts with my friends and family had been experiencing delays all afternoon and evening. Our text communications were a constant source of valuable information from around the Houston area and boosted my morale. Dedra's texts were experiencing delays late in the evening as well. The interruption of the communication stream gave me a growing sense of our isolation. The gaps between the *radar-red-colored* bands of rain that assailed us were growing smaller in the night. The tide was coming in. Everything was lining up against us, against the city.

I walked down the back staircase by the garage, which connects an add-on above the garage and serves as a guest room and office. It is on a level a few steps below the rest of the upstairs. As I made my way around the tight turn of the staircase, I could see a flowing current coming from under the door. It was really streaming in now. I walked back up the steps to the upstairs and then back down the front staircase connecting the entryway to the upstairs, and serving as our decontamination chamber. I looked at my mark, which was underwater by four or more inches by now. It was 12:36 AM–less than an hour from my prior reading. The water was climbing three times faster than before!

My texting delays began to annoy me seriously at this point. Dedra was due with a creek reading. Brad had earlier texted videos to a group of friends of his deck, and the water creeping up on it from the bay. Still it rained harder. I went to the TV to see the latest radar images. Every time a radar-yellow (lighter) patch of rain would flow northward from the coast, it would blossom into a bright red patch right over Friendswood, and any other portion of the city suffering under the same band of thunderstorms. I opened the door to Alex's room, "Hey, we may need to execute a few procedures here in a bit."

"What?" he pulled his headphones off and looked a bit puzzled, perhaps by my role-playing lingo that he would have objected to anyway, if he had known what it was.

"At some point, we are going to have to manually shut down the electricity. I have developed a plan for doing it. But, I was really hoping to avoid it."

"What's the plan? I can do it," he volunteered. He was ready to engage in some storm action after watching it on TV and waiting out the days in his room.

"No, I'll do it. But I will need you to help me make sure the power goes off, and to call mom if something goes wrong. Not that anything will. The procedure was designed with crew safety at the paramount."

"Stop talking with the space stuff, will you? This is serious, Dad," he scolded me.

"It is. And we are addressing it in a serious

way," I retorted. "I just use the lingo to keep me focused and light. We have to have a plan for action in case the waters continue to rise regardless of the lingo. Electricity shut off is first. At this rate, we probably only have a couple of hours before the water gets into the outlets. We'll have to shut it off before then," I explained the plan.

"What happens if we don't? Will the house blow up?" he asked as his interest level continued to increase.

"No. It won't blow up," I assured him, not particularly sure whether the question was serious. "There is a small chance that the water could short a circuit when it comes in through the outlet and create an arc of electricity that could start a fire. Just a small chance–but I am not really comfortable taking any chances with a potential for fire."

"Let me do it. I can do it," he pleaded. No question he would have less anxiety about this operation than I would, given the exuberance of youth and his desire for action. But it was a procedure I had to conduct myself. I was the one that got us in this mess. If anyone had to step outside to face Harvey's rage, it had to be me.

"Just be ready for your role when it's time. And make sure Maggie is ok. We may have to float out of here tonight. That's Phase Two: If the water keeps rising, we evacuate to the HEB," I returned downstairs and saw the water continuing to flow into the house, pushing the French doors in back, open in the middle. The water was above my recent mark by two inches. 1:04 AM. It was coming in even faster! And the rain had not slowed a whit. I was going to have to execute the manual shut down sooner rather than later.

I was hoping for a less intensive period of rain during which to conduct the EVA to shut down power. I gave it a little more time, hoping for a break. As I waited for the deluge to give way to a more reasonable rainfall rate, I decided that the situation called for a moment of contemplation, and a large glass of Cabernet. I decided to accompany my contemplative preparation with a continuation of the 1970s theme with which I had begun the evening. ELO's *Showdown* seemed right for the occasion. The string chords in its intro set the tone, and I thought of the people who had climbed on rooftops, clung to pool toys, and been pulled up into a helicopter. My situation was relatively easy by comparison. Houstonians from all areas of the city were facing Harvey's nighttime wrath, holding their own, fighting back in their own ways. I sang out with the chorus.

> *There's gonna be a showdown,*
> *And it's raaaaining all over the wooooorld,*
> *It's raaaaining all over the wooooorld,*
> *Tonight, the longest night."*

I took a long swig of my wine, set the glass down, and made my way to the decontamination area. As I began to initiate the final preparations for the procedure, it dawned on me that the manual shutdown plan was developed, in its original inception, to be performed in the daytime. At night, I would need to hold a flashlight, which would mean I could not carry the bat with me. It suddenly occurred to me—the headband light! My last-minute purchase, a true gift from the Fates! I returned upstairs to grab it from the supply table.

I strapped on the headband light and tried out its settings. I adjusted its angle to give me a good radius of light in front of me. The headlight, like my own Phial of Galadriel, upon my head, and the liquid courage beginning to take effect, I was ennobled to conduct the procedure. I alerted Alex to the initiation of the procedure. Over his protestations, I gave him the role of lookout and reporter to next of kin, aka mom, if something unforeseen were to occur. I slipped on the heavy waders and secured them in place on my shoulders. The lights were still on in the entryway and living-room so I could see the water flowing into the house as I suited up. It was only an inch or so from the bottom outlet. I needed to pick up my pace.

I opened the package of kitchen rubber gloves, containing two pair of gloves. I put one pair on my hands and decided to place one of the gloves from the extra set over the handle end of the baseball bat to further insulate myself from any remote chance that a spark arch from the breaker box. When the time came to flip the switch, I would turn the bat around and use the rubberized hand-glove covered handle end to trip the switches. Admittedly, it made for a rather odd-looking tool, but I wasn't concerned with appearances at the time. I grabbed the stepladder, its metal frame was a concern, however, its steps and my boots were rubber, so I felt comforted.

Fully suited for conducting the EVA procedure, I stepped forth from the decontamination chamber and into the rising waters of the downstairs.

"I'm not going to tell you how ridiculous you look right now, but I do think your plan will work," Alex gave me words of encouragement tinged with teenage censure—both helped. "Good luck."

"It'll work," I replied with a wink and a nod, turning around to head toward the back door. "But stay upstairs and call Mom if it doesn't," I said walking away. "And let me know when the lights go out."

"Sure, but I have a feeling you'll know."

I opened inward the French doors connecting to the back patio, which had already been nudged open by the surging water. At least a half dozen water beetles swam in with the small wake created by the opening of the door. Ahead of me water poured from the eaves above the patio; the amount of rain far surpassing the capacity of the gutters. Sheets of water crashed upon the back of the LM and broke around its back. The sloshing and pounding rain sounded differently outdoors than it did inside, as if I could now hear the angry whispers amongst the stomping boots. All of my senses stood on edge as the lightning and thunder flashed and cracked in the sky above. "I should have had another glass of wine," I mumbled to myself.

I took a deep breath and lunged through the runoff-produced waterfall, expecting that it would give way to some lighter version of the downpour—like stepping through a portal into another dimension. But if the deluge were less, it was not by much. The water soaked me from above and splashed me from below. The headlamp combined with the still working bedroom light gave me some indication of my path through the yard and around the hedge. Still, it was difficult to discern anything beyond the six-foot radius of light provided by the headlight beam. And even within the radius of its aura, the constant rain and splashing of the floodwaters diffused and refracted the light to such an extent that it was difficult to discern anything with great confidence.

I made my wobbly way along the edge of the landscaping on the spongy turf. The water was at my waist and getting deeper as I worked my way farther from the patio. I held the bat above the water, while I lifted the stepladder aloft as best I could, dragging it through the water as I trudged forward. As I approached the shoulder-high hedges that provided cover for the pool pump and electrical box, the images revealed in the low, dancing light, gave me pause to give it wide berth. A softball size colony of fire ants was bobbing toward the hedge, with the closest ants beginning to cling to it for refuge. An array of insects and arachnids took refuge within the leaves and branches, as the tops of the tall hedges remained one of the few areas in the back yard not entirely underwater. I wanted nothing to do with any of them. I squeezed the rubber glove around the handle of the bat, making sure I was ready in case some more menacing creature lurked.

Zzzst—crack! The skies above lit up briefly and the thunder made an awful roar.

"Sweet Jesus!" It felt like I jumped nearly out of the suit, the shoulder straps the only thing keeping me in place. My heart raced. Just a few more steps, and I would be there. I tried to calm myself as Harvey continued to wail with flashes and bangs, furious that I dared to emerge into his presence. I felt with my boot for the pool pump hidden somewhere nearby under the murky waters. The waters were over waist high, and the stepladder was not going to keep me out of the water to conduct the procedure, at least not at a level I could safely be on a stepladder, on an uneven surface, in a driving rain, with a baseball bat in my hand, in a borrowed rubber suit, and with creepy crawly things abounding.

I made it to the electrical box and opened its large metal door. The rain pelted its top and poured over the edge with the same cascading effect as from the eaves of the house. Even if the circuits had been better marked, I could make out very little. The box held two main switches and several smaller ones controlling different areas of the house. I was not exactly sure which breaker controlled which area, so I decided to flip the main breakers first, and then just flip the smaller ones as a failsafe.

Against the Storm

I set up the stepladder at least to give myself a higher angle for flipping the switches, even if my feet would still be in the water. I took one step up on it and nervously switched my hold on the bat from the glove covered handle, to the larger barrel. I reached out with the glove-covered tip of the bat handle toward the first of the main switches, and pushed the bat with a force to flip the switch into the off position. It flipped with a flash of rapidly vanishing light from the upstairs and a muffled pop. One down.

I heard sounds from the upstairs window, but I could not make the words. Alex was yelling something.

I stepped down and made my way back to the side of the house to see if I could make out what he was saying. The bedroom light was still on, lighting the turning point in the yard.

"What?" I yelled toward the now-dark window blurred by the cascading water from the eaves.

"Lights are out upstairs," he yelled back.

I did ask him to tell me. "Ok. Going to flip the second switch," I yelled back, turning around.

"What?" he replied, unclear on my response.

I just kept moving back toward the breaker box, my footsteps increasingly heavy as the waders were taking on water. My sock covered feet were submerged within the suit giving them the feel that they were at one with the waters outside them. I took a step up on the stepladder and flipped the second main switch with the same flash and muffled pop effect as the first, except this time it left the back

117

yard entirely dark. While I cannot say exactly where the water level was in the house at the time I finally completed the procedure, for purposes of the retelling of this story, I will take liberty to suggest that the water had reached the very lip of the outlets, beginning to trickle into the casing with the electrically charged wires. My deactivation happened just as the water was making contact with the wire, right in the nick of time, as if the time on the villain's bomb had reached 0:01.

I heard Alex's muffled yell again, undoubtedly fulfilling his role as requested. I flipped all the smaller switches as planned, and began to make my way back to the house. On the return, I had only the six-foot radius of light from the headlamp to guide me as the house was now cloaked in absolute darkness. I worked my way back a good distance from the hedge, and whatever it held in its shadows. I had turned the bat back around to serve its primary security function, and I had left the stepladder behind me at the breaker box. I moved as quickly as I could in the driving rain in the increasingly heavy EVA suit, the water inside of it at my ankles.

I glanced all around me as I walked, my head movements giving direction to the light. Where it shone, I could make out vague things. Where it did not, there was darkness. Complete, unnatural, and unnerving darkness. Various detritus would emerge into the radius of light from the darkness without warning, providing a rush to the senses as the newly lit debris could be discerned. Twigs, leaves, woodchips, and unsecured pool tools would present themselves into my tiny field of lighted vision from the rainy darkness and give me anxious moments of calculation as my mind gave meaning to the newly illuminated shapes. Thusly, I made my way back onto the patio and toward the back door. The shadows of the patio and house shifted with my moving head, mixing greys and blacks in an eerie display. I had made it under the eave, and out from the heavy rain and flashing skies, though they still rumbled behind me as I approached the back door.

"Son of a – !" *Sploosh*! I swung the bat quickly at the narrow black object that floated into my light radius. After my wild swing I took a stumbling step back to try to relocate the snake's position.

"What?! What?!" Alex yelled out from above, concern in his voice.

I readied the bat for a second swing. I saw what now was more clearly the toe of one of my black dress socks. "It's a sock," I called out. "It's just a freaking sock," I muttered to myself, still surging with adrenaline. I grabbed the sock and threw it outside into the back yard, as if it were one of Harvey's minions and not my own fear to blame. But fear was Harvey's greatest weapon. I felt it. Many throughout the city, in this long night felt it.

I climbed up into the entryway decompression chamber. I wormed my way out of the heavy waders and dumped the water that was filling them into the downstairs flood waters. The

119

Greg Etzel

waters in the house had risen to the level of the outlets, and the unceasing rains only increased the flow. I took off the gloves, laid the bat down on the antique table we had pulled out of the dining room and onto the entryway, and dried myself off.

"I think I will have that glass of wine now," I said, exhausted, but satisfied that the procedure was a success. "Well, there were no sparks. The house didn't start burning. All troops accounted for. So, I think we can call that mission a success."

"Yes," Alex said, and with an ominously accurate observation. "Congratulations, now we get to face Harvey in the dark."

120

X. The Abyss

We stood in the entryway, the lamp on my head the only instrument challenging the darkness that had enveloped us. The murky floodwaters rippled beneath. The storm pounded above. In between, Alex and I stood facing each other, our shelter shrinking and unlit. The shadows from my headlamp gave unusual shapes to the objects with which my mind had long grown familiar. It was as if we had been transported into another world.

We made our way up the staircase and sat at the TV room command bar table. I turned off my light to let our eyes attempt adjust to the darkness. Mine did not adjust well and contrasts between dark grey and black were all that governed my discernment. Our mood had changed as much as the lighting in our shelter. The mixed levity and active efforts to combat the storm in the relative comfort of lit surroundings had yielded to a tone more reflective of the darkened surroundings. In darkness, the imagination takes control. The worries in our minds cast their own shadows among the darkened objects and gave substance to the unshapen figures of fear and doubt that Harvey had released.

"What's next?" Alex asked with nervous anticipation.

"We ride it out up here," I said, fighting to maintain confidence in our plan. "We still have plenty of time before we have to evacuate on the air mattress. We don't know what we'll face in the dark of night. So, we stay here until we're forced to abandon ship." I reached for my phone and unplugged it from the no longer functioning charger. It was at 96% battery, and it was anyone's guess how long it would last. I made sure my apps were closed and checked my texts. Dedra had reported the latest creek reading.

"Over 16 feet," I said aloud.

"Is that bad?" Alex inquired in response.

"Well, it ain't good," I said in my native-Texan tongue, following with a more optimistic, "It's the highest that it's been, but, the creek may not be rising at the same rate as it did the other day. So, I think we have some time." I looked at the time. It was nearing 2 AM. "You should try to get a little rest. I'll watch the waters for a while."

He took a flashlight and checked on Maggie, who was nervously laying on her bed. They kept each other company, if not easing each other's worries, at least sharing them. I poured that glass of wine I had been craving since venturing out into Harvey's thunderous rains. I took a gulp and thought of the bravery of countless soldiers, who must venture into opposing fire or sustain artillery barrages again, and again, and again. My trials were so trivial by comparison that I chuckled at the anxious tension that had built up within me during the procedure, and from which I was now recovering with a glass of Cabernet in the relative comfort of at least a roof over my head. Nevertheless, I continued the post-shut down relaxation process with full acceptance that I was not qualified to be a soldier. My admiration for them only deepened further by my acknowledgement.

I pondered our situation and imagined what others throughout the city must be going through. The TV that had been our constant companion and connection to the city was now off. In the city, the dramatic stories would continue to play out throughout the night, though we were no longer connected to them, buoyed by them. We were isolated now.

After a few more sips, I turned my headlamp back on and made my way to the back staircase to assess the progress of the water's rise. As I turned the tight corner on the stairwell, they greeted me— two Texas-sized tree roaches caught in the glare of my headlamp. One was on the third step up from the bottom of the stairs, the other was on the wall of the staircase separating it from the kitchen/breakfast area. In a stroke of good fortune, my flip-flops were just beneath me on one of the large triangular stair steps where the narrow staircase makes its 180-degree turn, and the steps widen to provide for the sharp change of direction. The sudden glare of the beam had caused them to begin to scurry away from the light, in opposite directions.

The one on the wall began to ascend higher, while the one on the step made its way to the edge and began scurrying upwards searching for a crevice. If there was unity in their motion, it was only in their avoidance of a path back to the floodwater from which they came. I reached down swiftly, grabbing the implement of their doom. My glance down to snag the flip-flop had given the cover of darkness to their scurries, but with strategic glances about with my head, my headlamp soon found the one on the wall moving along at an angle only slightly steeper than the stairs. Target acquired, the full toe-end of the flip flop was brought to bear on the vile creature, crushing his guts upon the wall.

"That's for Alicia!" I shouted, in vindication of the familial scars left decades ago.

I then quickly turned my head and light to the other foul creature. Unable to find a crevice while working its way along and up the stairs, it crept upwards at the very edge of the wall. The angle of the wall where it met the step spared the fearsome insect from my first blow. It scurried up the stair after it avoided the initial volley of slapping rubber, but my headlamp followed its every move. It would not escape me. Not this time. I decided to change my tactical approach given the roach's position on the edge of the step and wall, and opted for the *jab and crush* method. It worked with deadly efficiency. I left Harvey's vanquished minions where they lay as warnings to others who might seek to invade my upstairs domain. Whatever past demons I may have conquered in the scuffle, the victory felt hollow. The momentary boost in morale did nothing to ease a deepening doubt.

Nor did it stop the rain. All I could do was

watch the water rise. I had given up on marking the wall anymore, unable to find my Sharpie. I kept track by measuring how the water was progressing up the steps, and just estimated the time and flow rate. The storm fatigue had sapped my earlier desire for exactitude, and I settled for reasonable guesses. The water was clearly rising–up to the second step now—and the flow was steadily coming in from under the garage door, but the rise wasn't as fast as the first six-inch plus per hour surge. I went back into the office area atop the garage and checked my messages. Dedra had texted the latest creek measurement. Still going up, but the rate did not have the angle of rise that the initial flooding from two days ago had.

I called her, for the comfort of her voice more than anything else. I thanked her for the creek data and let her know that Alex was asleep with Maggie in his room while I was watching and waiting.

"Joanne and Robert are high and dry. If you can get to their house, they said you guys are welcome to stay there as long as you need." She had been in contact with our longtime friends, who had offered shelter in their new home in Friendswood a few miles up FM 528, where it was apparently not flooded. We have known Joanne and Robert since their youngest son and our oldest son attended pre-kindergarten, and I was grateful for their generosity.

"We'll see how the night goes," I said, knowing that no evacuation attempt would be possible until morning. We said our goodbyes, and I paced back and forth across the upstairs and halfway down the back stairwell and up again. Over and over, helplessly watching. The water was well above a foot and rising; the outlets were now underwater and the unmoved contents of the bottom 14 inches of our house began to float in defiance of the storage places to which we had assigned them. Harvey haphazardly sloshed our belongings about, covering them with his silty stench.

     I walked back to the front entryway, now within a few inches of being overtaken by the waters. I picked up the EVA suit and decided to take a walk around the flooded downstairs to assess the damage and to pass the time. Another tree roach scurried away as I lifted the hip waders from the floor. I stomped at the roach with my sock-covered foot, but it scampered into the entryway closet under the cover of darkness and soccer cleats. I decided to let it be, for now. I turned the hip-waders upside down and shook them violently, ensuring that no other enemy lie in wait for me as I made my walk around. Nothing crawled or fell out. I put the suit on and began to wade through the rooms amidst the debris. Harvey had made my downstairs his own, shifting pieces of furniture now with his water's whim.

     The eerie shadows and glare from the headlamp hitting the brown water did nothing to resolve my growing unease. Every piece of furniture, every cabinet, every corner produced shadows that slithered out of the way of my roaming beam. When I turned my head, it seemed that silent shadowy figures sleeked away, one step ahead of the light and into the darkness just beyond its edge. They lurked around the periphery of my small radius of light, repositioning themselves just beyond my perception. I was surrounded by them, but protected from their incursion by my headlamp, which chased them away with every turn, though often revealing spiders and waterbugs and other debris in the shadows' wake.

The French doors in back had been pushed wide open by the rising waters. Harvey had forced himself into the hearth of my home. Those shadows surrounding me were mere reminders of his presence. I stared out the open doors at the FJ Cruiser I had parked on the patio. The water had risen well above the exhaust pipe and wheels, rendering it incapable of starting. I again saw the unceasing rain pouring off the eaves, glistening in the light of my headlamp against the dark backdrop of the stormy night. It was as if I were once again staring back into the total eclipse. Harvey had forced himself into my head as much as into my home. In my fatigue, he now confronted me as I had confronted the sun a week ago.

"The rain comes when it comes," I muttered aloud, the farmer's simple wisdom. Desolate thoughts invaded my mind. I had invited myself to peer into the totality and to ponder my place among the sun, the Earth, the moon, and the stars. I could not *un-ask* the question. I had stared into the abyss and it stared into me. What did I see? What did *it* see?

The sun, the Earth, and the moon all continued to move on their paths, no longer aligned, but still constantly revolving and rotating through space and time. The universe unfolded around me, spinning into infinity. And there I stood, alone, on my patio staring into the driving rain, just a minute spec in its vastness. "The rain comes when it comes." Whatever I do, I cannot stop it. NASA can predict the eclipse, but they cannot prevent it from occurring. The laws of nature have been set in motion. They cannot be undone. Who am I to stand against them? What fool am I to have challenged the storm?

"The rain comes when it comes." My control was an illusion. My procedures just coping mechanisms. The agents of despair were revealing the vanity and futility of my actions, of any action, against them. There is no shield against the infinite —no aegis to block Harvey's blows. The waters will rise until they stop. We can run. We can float. But the rain comes when it comes. And it continued to come. I stared out into the night philosophically musing the helplessness of my state.

Yet, I fought back against Harvey's darkest forces of despair. I had to believe that it could not possibly keep raining like it was. The rain *had* to stop. The waters did seem to be rising more slowly than an hour ago. The floods were now likely expanding more widely into Friendswood, growing out more than up. If this were the case, it could at least buy us some time. Only a few hours until dawn, and the tide would begin to roll out, weakening Harvey's retaining forces. All of these thoughts gave me strength to continue standing before Harvey.

Still, the waters rose. The rains gave no consideration to my introspection. Harvey demanded full submission.

I broke my gaze from the storm and meandered through the shadowy world that once was my downstairs, thoughts much deeper than the floodwaters streamed through my head. I had to continue my watch, to make sure we were ready to float our way to high ground if our situation came to that. I walked up the back staircase and slipped out of the EVA suit at the turning steps, and went into the office where the air mattress sat, fully inflated.

I felt a combination of fatigue and anxiousness. My tired mind continued to wrestle with the heavier thoughts Harvey had forced upon me. I grabbed the bottle of Cabernet and brought it with me into the office above the garage. I placed it on the windowsill after filling up my half-empty glass, and sat down on the floor, leaning my back up against my desk, and I stared out the window. I still had at least a few hours before I would need to consider the air mattress escape plan. Memories of distant times and places began to drift in and out of my mind. I wanted to find comfort in them, but found only contemplation. What would they all come to? How would this unfold? What *did* I see?

Greg Etzel

"The rain comes when it comes," I said aloud, raising my glass in toast to the wisdom of farmers. It was only now that their words truly sank in. Only now that I could clearly see their understanding of nature's control. Farmers know. They build their farm towns around churches because they know that belief is all you have when the world lies beyond your control. Farmers know. My weary contemplations carried me heavily through the passing time, as I gazed out into the ever-pouring rains.

The rain had now adopted a steady pace. It was the pace of an advancing army, one that had broken the enemy line and was securing its gains. It showed no signs of stopping. Harvey did not care what *I* believed. Harvey only rained. No solace in his skies, no mercy in his murky waters. Against the infinite of the abyss, I was reduced to nothing. I slumped in my seated position, the weight of defeat heavy on my shoulders. My fatigue gained ground as my anxiousness melted into acceptance.

A tree roach had crawled its way onto the windowsill and up on to my wine glass. I did nothing as it perched on the edge of my glass, robbing from me the little comfort I had afforded myself in my crouched spot on the floor. I could not help but laugh, if only to keep from tears. Harvey sought to make a toast to his victory with the same wine that was delivered to my door before his arrival. I sat, slumped and exhausted, without the will to stop him. I felt utterly vanquished.

Against the Storm

I yearned for nothing now but sleep. I mustered as much will as I had to swat the roach away, not even caring to chase it and crush it for the insult it had visited upon me. I pushed the glass farther away from me on the windowsill and took a swig straight from the bottle. It was nearly 4 AM, and I decided that, given the rate of rise for the last hour, I had several hours before the water could make its way up the stairs to my level. In any event, my exhaustion compelled me to try to rest my anxious mind.

I checked my messages one last time and decided to lull myself into sleep with a song. With the old classics from the earlier evening in my mind, I turned to Paul Simon again for an old tune that spoke to me in the moment. To the soft tone of his melody and the contemplative poetry of his lyrics, I let my own anxious mind wind down. The storm swirled around me, the rains unremitting. I let the music lull me into slumber as I yearned for dawn as Simon sang:

> *And so, I'll continue to continue to pretend*
> *That my life will never end,*
> *And that flowers never bend*
> *With the rainfall.*

XI. Rescue & Retreat

It had only been a brief slumber, but the difference in the light of the early morning when I awoke and the darkness of the depth of night when I had drifted to sleep made it seem infinitely longer. The daylight and the much gentler rainfall did more to rejuvenate me than any rest I may have obtained slumped against my desk. I rose stiffly to my feet, aching in nearly every part of my body. I checked on Alex and Maggie, who were still fast asleep, seemingly oblivious to any existential crisis that may have been occurring around them. I walked to the stairwell and stepped into the EVA suit. The water had worked its way up the bottom 3-4 steps, and I descended downstairs to assess the situation in the lighter skies and brighter mood of the morning.

About two feet of floodwater sloshed about as I waded through the house. The unfamiliar shadow-world from only a few hours ago had given way to more familiar shapes. But it only revealed more clearly the extent of the disarray. Harvey claimed the downstairs as his own, shifting furniture and other contents at his arbitrary will. Each piece of furniture became an island in Harvey's sea. They played host to millipedes, doodle bugs, water beetles, spiders—many varieties of creepy-crawly things—all seeking refuge on the dry surfaces offered by the furniture.

In the light of the new morning, they seemed

less the minions of Harvey than fellow survivors. For millions of years their species have fought the arbitrary forces of nature, and they have thrived. In this great battle against Harvey's caprice, we were on the same side. I also saw a good number of lizards finding refuge, who would undoubtedly feast on the cornucopia presented before them. I was perfectly happy for now to allow the living room ecosystem to develop its own delicate balance among the competing species. Now, don't get me wrong, I still crushed every cockroach I could find. They'll need millions more years of adaptation to survive the lethality of a flip-flop.

I kept my eye out for ant-balls and snakes. Every sock was a lesser suspect in the daylight, and I was fortunate not to find any other signs of serpent reptiles. I was not overly concerned about the other, far scarier, local reptile whose range can be expanded with the swelling creeks. Alligators were scarce around this part of Clear Creek, but in many flooded homes throughout the outlying areas of Houston, they were quite rationally feared by homeowners wandering around in the floodwaters of their property.

Everywhere there was debris, either from inside the house or from the outdoors, bobbing lifelessly on calm waters. The water had stopped rising while I slept, and it settled into an equilibrium, my footsteps creating the only ripple and flow. I made my way outside and into the back yard. In the light gray sky and sprinkling rain, it too bore no resemblance to itself only a few hours ago when lightning flashed in the darkness above and claps of thunder accompanied the hammering of the rain. Darkness is fear's greatest weapon. The water was waist deep as I made my way toward the front of the house.

As I walked, I heard the low hum of an engine coming from down the street. I looked back and saw an airboat heading up what was once a street in my direction. Three individuals rode in the boat–the driver, another man standing next to him, and an older woman who sat crouched on a bench under an umbrella. They pulled up near me in my front yard.

"You doin' ok?" they yelled out to me, above the din of their engine.

"Yeah, we survived the night all right," I responded as he cut his engine. He drifted closer to me, looking down from his boat as his co-pilot moved toward the side of the boat and spoke out to me.

"You need a ride out?" he asked. "We need to run her up the street to the truck first. But we're coming back this way."

"Thanks, have they said anything about the rain? Is it moving out?" I inquired, my information more limited now as I tried to preserve my phone's battery.

"Not sure. Could be another 18 inches."

Eighteen more inches of rain? I pondered to myself, how could there be 18 inches of rain left in the skies? Had they not all poured out by now? I had the provisions, I could last this out if the rain would just stop. The morning had renewed my will to fight, but another heavy assault and we would be flushed out. Though I debated internally, in all honesty, I knew as soon as I heard the airboat's engine what the decision would be. It was time to concede.

Many years ago, I was on a church council. I generally had responsibilities for promoting stewardship, and, on occasion, I would be asked to speak to the congregation to promote some program or another. I generally liked to start them with a bit of humor, so I would blatantly plagiarize any old saw that would remotely align with the theme of the message and kick off the talk with it. Once, I began with this old fable; forgive me if you've heard it before.

Once, a faithful man lived in a house by the river. It was said he trusted God in all things. One day the rains came, and he prayed to be saved from the storm. When the rains kept coming, his neighbors offered to drive him out. But he stayed.

"The Lord will save me," he said.

When the rains kept coming, and the waters rose to man's doorstep, he prayed again. The rains kept coming, and the town's sheriff rode out in a boat to give him passage to shelter. The faithful man, thanked the sheriff and sent him on his way.

"The Lord will save me," he said.

The faithful man continued to pray as he climbed onto his roof to avoid the water's continued

135

rise. A national guard helicopter flew overhead and tossed a line to him. He bid the copter to continue on its way.

"The Lord will save me," he said.

The faithful man drown moments later when the river's waters washed him away. When he arrived in heaven, because he had lived such a good and faithful life, he was granted one question of God. He seized the opportunity, saying, "Lord, I was a good and faithful man. I kept to my prayers and pled for you to save me. Why didn't you save me?"

The Lord looked down to the good man and said, "Well, I sent a truck, a boat, and helicopter.... "

Now, as blunt an object as my mind may be, even it was capable of deciphering the meaning of a message when presented within the exact literal context of the parable itself. As soon as I heard the engine's hum, I knew we had to take the boat out of here, away from our home. No way am I being hoisted into a helicopter; I'm not a big fan of heights, after all. Harvey would get the submission he desired.

"I have son and a dog with me. Can you take us? I'll have us ready when you get back," I asked the rescuer.

"You got it, buddy." He fired up the engine and began to maneuver the boat up the canals that our neighborhood streets had become. He headed back toward the front of the neighborhood where the waters did not reach.

I scampered as quickly as I could in the near

Against the Storm

chest deep water toward the front door of the house to get Alex and Maggie. The rear door to the Honda Pilot was fully open, having shorted out with the waters that poured into the vehicle's cabin. All around me was Clear Creek, as broad as the eye could see, houses popping out of its murky brown surface like a chain of islands. I clambered up the steps to the house.

"Alex! Wake up! Alex!" I yelled out as I ran upstairs to his room, fully suited in the hip waders "Evacuation time!" I roused him awake. "Grab a change of clothes. I'll get a bag." I rushed out as quickly as I rushed in.

"Wait, what?" he was groggily getting to his feet and trying to understand the frenzied situation to which he had awoken.

"There's a rescue boat coming. It will be here in five minutes. Pack up and bring Maggie," I gave him the vital parts, and spun out of the room to get a bag.

"A rescue boat?" Alex was still perplexed but gathered himself, his clothes and Maggie.

I grabbed Maggie's food, her leash, four bottles of water, a couple of items of spare clothing, a charger and stuffed them in a bag before returning to Alex's room to add whatever he had gathered. It was admittedly a bit of a mad scramble. I threw the bag's strap over my shoulder and led the way downstairs and out the front door. Alex was carrying a completely compliant, but entirely nervous Maggie in his arms at his waist.

137

Greg Etzel

Alex waded into the waters slowly, recoiling at the cold feel of the rainwater swollen creek. He lacked the hip waders that I had on, and made his way cautiously into the deeper water. He had to hoist Maggie higher with each step, her nervousness increasing until she released the entire contents of her extremely full bladder into the water directly in front of Alex. Indeed, as later examination of Alex's room would indicate, it may have been the first time she had been to the bathroom in nearly two days. Literally and figuratively, Alex took it in stride, though the look on his face likely matched my own when the cockroach hoisted itself up on my wine glass.

I helped him with Maggie as the water got deeper as we neared the rescue boat. We climbed onboard the boat, with no small degree of difficulty.

"Thank you," I said to our rescuer gratefully as he pulled us in. I asked him and his friend their names, but in the chaos and exhaustion of that day and the many to follow, I have forgotten them. Though it was clear they were not doing this because they wanted us to remember their names. They were just doing what they felt they had to do. Something within their own being drove them to help rescue us and countless others.

Now, by rescuer, I do not mean to imply that they were police or fire department rescue workers or members of the national guard. They were one of the many hundreds (if not thousands) of *guys with boats* throughout the Houston area that had been working for two and half days in ridiculous conditions to save people from Harvey's rising floodwaters. Just groups of average guys with boats patrolling neighborhoods and pulling people out of high waters and on to higher ground so they could find shelter. *The Cajun Navy* became the colloquial term for these heroic citizens. May history remember their deeds.

The driver cranked up the engine, its giant propeller spinning rapidly in its metal cage, and we began to turn away from the house. I felt utterly defeated. We were retreating from the field of battle, surrendering to Harvey that which we had pledged to defend. This was not how it was supposed to end when I formulated the plan during my jog days ago. But as I knew now, this is how it always ends when you challenge Mother Nature—in retreat. In defeat.

We skimmed the water as we moved along the flooded road, the rain picking up as we went. We reached the front part of the neighborhood, where we helped them move the airboat onto a trailer on the back of the boat driver's truck. They were moving to another neighborhood to answer another call for help. They had been doing this for the better part of two days. We climbed in the bed of the pickup truck and made the ride out of our neighborhood on their way to the next stranded survivor. They were going to drop us off at the nearby grocery store, where we would call Joanne to arrange for transport to their house once the roads were clear.

We made it out of our neighborhood on a relatively dry patch of road before hitting high water just one neighborhood over. The water was passable for our rescuer's large truck, but not many other vehicles. Someone standing outside the neighborhood stopped them to ask them a question. I didn't pick up the conversation, but it had something to do with an elderly lady down the street. The rescue guys hopped out of the truck and said they were going to check on this lady. I offered to assist. I think he saw that I needed him to accept the offer more for my sake than his. They likely didn't need my efforts, but I needed to help them in any way I could as a token of my gratitude for the help they offered me. He assisted me off the back of the truck, graciously accepting my symbolic offering.

It was quite undramatic, as is it turned out. We walked down the street, as the water was just at the threshold of several houses in the front of the subdivision and any wake from passing boats would slosh waves of water into their homes. The lady in question did not yet have water in her house and indicated she had plenty of supplies. So, we walked back to the truck and boat, the two rescuers grumbling like a trauma team that was called from an amputation to attend to a broken finger. I was just happy to tag along.

On our walk, he described some of the rescues they had performed as well as ones that other *Cajun Navy* boaters had made. He said that on that day more National Guard and emergency agencies, state and federal, were coming in to assist. Harvey had triggered a full-on military intervention by the most powerful nation in the world. The United States Marine Corps were en-route to Friendswood, Texas! The cavalry was on its way!

And while everyone was relieved that more help was coming in, I caught a slight tinge of *we got this* pride as we walked. He told of a story of a group of Federal Emergency Management Agency rescue boat operators who arrived at a large neighborhood to begin extraction missions and found a group of *Cajun Navy* boaters shuttling people from the back of the flooded neighborhood to the front where they could be transported to drier ground. The lead FEMA team member asked one of the boaters, "What agency are 'you guys' with?" Our rescuer laughed, and retold the response as, "There ain't no agency out here; we're just a bunch of guys with boats." I laughed myself at his retelling, imagining the Texas independent spirit oozing from every word. Indeed, we would hear tales of monster trucks coming to the rescue of stranded national guard vehicles. I know of simply nothing more Houston than that.

Yet, I think, truth be told, he would have been the first to tell anyone, they were glad the big guns had arrived to help. I enjoyed his stories, for the brief time he had to share them on our walk back, I climbed into the back of the bed of the truck with Alex and Maggie who had sat despondently in the rain the entire time.

Our rescuers dropped us off at the nearby HEB on the way to their next extraction mission. I regret that I have forgotten their names, but I'm forever grateful for their anonymous gift. I am testimony to their efforts, and to the efforts of the hundreds, if not thousands, of *guys with boats* who made a silent contribution to the history of Houston. Perhaps it is overly dramatic to compare it to *Dunkirk,* but the nobility of conscious of the common man shined brightly against Harvey's dark forces and many real lives were spared by their virtue during the days of the flood. The spirit of Houston was a lamp for all to see.

Rescued though we were, we were now refugees. I had surrendered our home to Harvey. We hopped out of the truck and stood briefly in the parking lot before wandering under the covered area just outside the grocery store door. We were a most pathetic looking threesome. Soaked to the bone, unkept matted wet hair dripping, exhausted blank faces, standing lifelessly while the light rain spat upon us. I took in the moment, and from it hoped to retain the sense of humility it impressed upon me.

Around us was the surreal. The parking lot was virtually empty, all of the businesses closed and lifeless. Large military vehicles were coming up from the Alvin direction of FM528 and moving toward the direction of Clear Creek. All of the drainage ditches around the parking lot were overflowing and draining rapidly toward the direction of the creek. Debris lay scattered about where Harvey had left it. Above us the sound of military and rescue helicopters began to hum. Alex looked up to me, the water from his hair streaming down his face, the smallest trace of a muted grin in his cheek.

"Do you think they'll cancel school tomorrow?"

XII. What Will Tomorrow Bring?

We didn't have to wait long in the HEB
parking lot. Joanne and Robert came practically as
soon as they got the call. They lived just a few miles
west on FM528, the same direction from which the
military vehicles were coming. FM 528 was
impassible to the east, rendering traffic to and from
Houston via that road impossible. The other main
highway, FM518, was also impassible in both
directions, north and south. Friendswood had
become a virtual island, besieged by the many
creeks that traversed it. Yet its situation was no
different than that of thousands of neighborhoods
and communities throughout Houston.

Reservoirs overflowed, bayous spilled into
crowded urban areas, vehicles and homes were
submerged throughout the city. At area hospitals,
staff stayed on working in emergency shifts to cover
for health care workers who couldn't get in to relieve
them. Everywhere emergency personnel worked
virtually without sleep for three days just getting
people to shelter or taking care of them in shelters.
Demands for supplies at shelters began to increase.
The city was in a crisis. We, too, it seemed were in a
crisis.

Joanne and Robert graciously welcomed us
into their nice, comfortably dry, car. As we climbed in
the back seat, Maggie's nervousness from the
absolute whirlwind of a day she was having finally

culminated in the spontaneously delivery of an unsavory package right on the car seat. I quickly grabbed the product of her anxiety, with my bare hand, and placed it on the towel that Joanne had given me. Joanne and Robert laughed it off, while I cringed. I was so grateful for their compassion that I wanted to do nothing that would cause them further disruption. And lo and behold, my dog pooped on their nice leather car seat the instant I get in their car! No insult was beneath Harvey.

But neither Joanne nor Robert saw anything as disruption. Quite to the contrary, they opened their hearts and their home to us. They had just moved into a new house, different from the house we had visited over the years, although it was still in Friendswood. They had been there only a day or so before the storm, and were themselves in the middle of unpacking and getting internet and cable services connected at the house (all of which were delayed by the storm). They began to apologize for the chaotic status of things, but we all recognized that chaos was a more relative term than ever around town these days. They fed us, gave us a warm shower, and a warm bed. That was all we wanted for in the world at that moment.

We bivouacked at Robert and Joanne's while we simply waited to see what would happen next. We were living in an unprecedented state, taking things on a moment-to-moment basis. I was communicating with folks at my work and family members letting them know our status. My mother wanted us to come to her nearby, but unflooded, house as soon as the roads would allow it. We decided that we would meet Dedra and the twins there once the highways cleared. We really didn't know what the next day would bring. Harvey had undermined our most basic daily assumption – he had rendered us without a home.

My submission complete, Harvey began to move northeast and away from the Houston area, spreading his destruction wider. But at least he was going *away*. The Houston area had seen enough. The adjectives used by weathercasters and scientists to describe Harvey's rains would seem hyperbolic had I not witnessed the storm myself. The Earth's crust in the greater Houston area actually sank by two centimeters due to the sheer volume of water dropped upon it! Nearly 33 trillion gallons of water were estimated to have fallen from the sky during those few days before the rains finally stopped. The *entire* Harris county map *averaged* over three feet of rainfall over those two-plus days. And that was just the *average* rainfall for the county. Some areas, like Friendswood, received over 50 inches of rain. Harvey's rains stood alone atop all storms. And now my city and I stood pummeled in his wake.

We stayed the full day and night at Robert and Joanne's new house waiting for the waters to recede. I was unable to nap in the morning for very long, my mind racing to figure out what to do next. It felt helpless to sit still. Robert offered to drop me off near our neighborhood, as close as his car could get, on his way to their former house, where he was going to pick something up to bring to the new house. I pulled the EVA suit out of his trunk, stepped into it, and trudged back to the house eager to do something other than wait. I felt like a scavenger coming back to the scene of a lost battle. I rummaged around just to get a general assessment of the damage. I began taking pictures to document the loss. I also wanted to bring something for Robert and Joanne as a token offering for the Mexican dinner Joanne had planned for the evening.

Joanne had been with Dedra on the girl's trip to Napa, and had purchased a bottle from a vineyard that Robert and Joanne really liked. I knew I had a Pinot Noir from that vineyard above the bar. I grabbed it and stuffed it in my EVA suit, feeling that I was looting from Harvey's spoils. After ambling through the mess further without any real utility, I began the long walk back to meet Robert. As I walked through the streets connecting our neighborhood to the next, there were very few signs of activity. Large trucks would traverse the deeper waters that isolated neighborhood from neighborhood. In between, a few folks in golf carts were patrolling the dry pockets, one with a shotgun racked in the back. Looters beware, I thought, as I nervously considered the bottle of Pinot Noir nudged inside my EVA suit between my hip and the inside of the suit. I walked past the local self-appointed legal authority, exchanging a friendly "Howdy" as he drove by. Despite knowing that the wine was my own, I had an internal recognition that I was wandering in a time and place that may have been somewhat extra-judiciary. Nevertheless, my spoils seemed secure.

I reconnected with Robert and returned to their home, where we passed the time in good company, and relatively good spirits, with a bottle of Pinot Noir and enchiladas. Even if it had not been preceded with several straight meals of bean dip and salsa, it would have been a delicious Texas meal. Its warmth and comfort matched that of our gracious hosts. It was a delightful distraction, and together with the clearing skies, it kept our spirits from lagging further.

When my cell phone signal would permit, I checked on the Astros as a distraction from my own struggles. I discovered that they too had been displaced by the storm—forced to play a three-game *home* stand against the Rangers in Tropicana Field in Florida. In front of a tiny crowd of a few thousand people, they were playing like a team lost in the wake of a storm. Their August struggles seemed to reach a climax with a bruising ten-run loss that evening. It would be followed the next day with another big loss; the Astros' ace pitcher giving up six earned runs. It seemed we were unraveling together.

For us at least, the next day brought better weather. Dedra had found a route that would bring her to my mother's house in Pasadena from Dallas without encountering any road closures. We could reconnect with them there that night, *if* we could find a way across the creeks. The skies were finally clearing behind Harvey and the waters were beginning to recede to the point at our house where I could test the FJ Cruiser. Robert dropped me off, much closer to the house this time, as the waters had made substantial retreat in the overnight hours. After a bit of a sputter, the FJ Cruiser cranked to life. We had our LM back! I took it for a spin to see how the roads around the area looked.

I found the soaked remains of three abandoned vehicles revealed by the receding waters at the Coward's Creek bridge on FM518, over which the waters continued to flow, but now at much lower levels than the previous days. The same held true at the Chigger Creek crossing, though fewer washed-out cars were left in the shrinking floodwaters. Both ways were still impassible, even in the FJ Cruiser, but they were significantly lower than their high-water mark. It was more of the same as I drove east on FM528 to the large bridge over Clear Creek. The waters still stretched wide, but they too had receded greatly as evidenced by the *No Wake* signs littered along now-dry parts of the highway. The flooded seven-lane highway had been a major channel for rescue boat traffic on the preceding days, and the nearby businesses had placed the signs along the Venetian-styled expressway to reduce the waves sloshing into their offices. Given the location of the signs from what was now the water's edge, the floodwaters did appear to be draining quickly.

As I waited for the waters to recede, I stopped by the local 24 Hour Fitness parking lot, which had been converted to a staging ground for a unit of US Marines equipped with large amphibious vehicles. Small crowds of residents, like myself, milled about taking pictures and thanking them for riding to the rescue. Limited supplies were being handed out there and at various other locations. Harvey's assault on Friendswood flooded one-third of the community's homes. One of every three people in town, stood like me, homeless, wandering, wondering where their next night's sleep would be spent. The community was organizing in relief with the assistance of help from all avenues. Indeed, Alex met with a group of his friends and then with the entire Friendswood High School Athletic program as they worked throughout the day mucking out houses in areas where the water had already receded.

Later in the day, I returned to the house to check on the waters and found my uncle, Glenn, parking his truck.

"How'd you get across the creek?" I was amazed to find him there.

"I came down 518. It's passable now." He got word via my mother that we were flooded out and was ready the second the roads between his home in League City and Friendswood opened to transport his generator to us. We unloaded it off the truck, and brought it to the back of the house. He brought me a hot lunch and said he was *ready to work* in the morning. I mentioned to him that our journey to see the eclipse, and his reminders during that event, had revitalized a connection in me with my grandfather in a way that directly inspired our preparation before, and procedures during, the storm. He smiled at my retelling of the tales. I smiled at his gracious offer of assistance and his empirical evidence of an open route out of town.

After bidding a warm thanks to Joanne and Robert, Alex and I reunited with Dedra, Grace, and Harry at my mother's house. Her house escaped any flooding and avoided most damage. She wanted us to stay in her house, which was about a 20-30 minute drive from our own, as long as we needed to get back on our feet. I just hoped the next day would bring the beginning of clean-up for us. We would plan on emptying out the downstairs of our soaked home as much as we could. In the meantime, my mother made us a nice dinner, and we shared Harvey stories. It was great to be all together again after being separated by the storm for five days.

Well, almost all together. Zach, who had kept connected throughout from his dorm setting in Tennessee, was with us in spirit. In fact, he now lay directly in the path of what remained of Harvey. Ultimately, Harvey would make his way through Texas and directly hit Memphis with the heavy rains of a tropical depression, soaking Zach with the same waters that had washed away the downstairs of his boyhood home. As it would turn out, Harvey expired as a storm on the very spot where I began my journey to face the sun a little more than a week before. It was an existential flourish worthy of theatrical applause. Were it not the truth, I couldn't have written it any better.

After a short time sharing stories with my family, I grew weary and wandered my way upstairs to go to bed. I could not help but think there was a reason Glenn was the first person I saw at our house once the storm had receded. Seeing him brought me back to the beginning, to Nebraska, where I stood aligned with the sun and the moon in the darkness of the middle of the day, stars and planets visible all around me. It was a reminder of the infinite musings that had accompanied my long journey home after standing in that alignment. It was a reminder that there was still a battle raging even though the rains had stopped. Questions far deeper than the floodwaters that invaded our home and that would not recede as rapidly. I was not yet finished. Only the rain had stopped.

I, too, was returning to where it all began – my boyhood home. I felt very much like I had 30 years ago, hovering on the brink of adulthood, not knowing what lay in store for me. Boyish hopes and fears long muted by the unfolding of time seemed brand new again. Harvey jarred me from routine and gave me cause to question my confidence in what tomorrow would bring. I lay in bed with a million and one thoughts racing through my mind.

Slowly, staring at the ceiling, or laying with my eyes closed, I began to give way to a restive state. As I began to fade, my mother's air conditioner kicked on with a noise that sounded like the start of a heavy rainfall. I jolted up, before recognizing the sound for what it was with my heart began racing as rapidly as my mind had previously. Harvey haunted me. I could still hear his rains in my head when I closed my eyes. After another lengthy period getting my heart to perform the same slowdown my brain had performed, and was again performing, I finally fell asleep.

That night I dreamt I was standing in the Nebraska cornfields again, staring into the eclipse, just like I had about ten days before. I saw the corona dancing around the deep blue-black shadow in the center of the moon-occluded sun. Like before, my eyes were drawn to it. This time, as I gazed, the center of the darkness moved closer and closer. As it moved toward me, water began to rise beneath me. The rising water spiraled around me, taking with it all of my belongings in a tortured flotilla into the center of the darkness. It spiraled continuously as I was drawn still closer toward the center. I was trapped in my position, limited even in my dream, to the small confines of time and space where I existed amidst the vastness of the universe.

I was confronted by the abyss again. Standing aligned with the sun and the moon, I recognized my insignificant presence on their epic scale. Their motion around me gave no heed to my existence and no concern to my will. Like Harvey's rains, they moved on their own course, set in motion long ago and dictated by natural laws beyond my capacity to change. I was reduced to a spec of nothingness in the Nebraska plains being swallowed by the abyss.

Then I remembered the horizon. A color existed in the brief moment of totality on the edge of the earth and sky. I broke my gaze from the totality and looked toward the horizon. Its orange-purple hue was unlike any I had ever seen. The indescribable beauty of that color spanned the entire 360-degree horizon, giving a sign that all was not consumed in darkness. Even in the shadow of the sun, light shimmered. However faint, its radiance was all the more alluring from the implicit promise it conveyed. Above me, the abyss churned in its infinity. I ran, fighting to keep my eyes focused on the horizon, sheltered in that soft orangish hue until it transformed into dawn.

The morning brought sunlight beaming in through the small gap in the curtains in my mother's guest room. In the beam of sunshine, small constellations of dust particles drifted in invisible currents of air. (For the record, Mother, they were only small dust constellations and only made visible by a beam of sunshine. Very small, I am only calling them out for dramatic effect here.) The sunlight was a welcome companion, particularly after my dream. I was heading back to our house early to begin tearing things out, while Dedra and the kids would join me a bit later.

My mother and sister's family were leaving early in the morning for a long-planned trip to Disney World. Despite the storm, their trip was on, although it would be rerouted with an additional eight hours of driving due to road closures. (In another twist of fate, they would end up needing to leave Orlando just before Hurricane Irma, the next storm, made her mark on Florida.) I saw them off and got on my way myself. I thought about my dream on the drive over, and continued to fight the remnants of Harvey in my head.

I found an open convenience store that had gasoline, but no ice. As I was filling up, a cardinal lighted on the shrubbery near the street. I smiled warmly. My mother once told me several years after my father's death that whenever she sees a cardinal, she knows that my father is still around looking after her. I thought it a sweet, sentimental gesture at the time. It was a clever tool, as I think of my father reflexively every time I see a cardinal. And, being that they are very common to the area, I practically see one every time I jog through Frankie Carter Randolph Park. Each time, it serves as a tangible reminder of the intangible feelings that remain, of the love that he shared that made me who I am. I saw a new wisdom in my mother's ways that morning.

The cardinal flew off quickly, but had served its purpose. Every day, as I raise four children of my own, I find myself more and more saying the things my father would have said, or doing things I said *I* would never do when *I* became a parent. My perspective changed, but the constancy of my father's presence has not. He would have *encouraged* my journey to see the eclipse; he would have *encouraged* my introspection. He didn't need to be here in person right now for me to know that he had lived, that he had loved, and that he had shaped me. His acts of love transcended time, surviving his death like an ever-present monument on the landscape of my being.

As I pulled into the neighborhood, I began to think of seeing Glenn yesterday, and appreciating the coincidence that he was the first I encountered at the house when the storm had subsided. It took me back to Nebraska before the storm was formed and reminded me I had experienced more than an eclipse. It was there where I was greeted with kindness and given a warm meal and a comfortable bed from family separated by generations of time and more than a thousand miles of geographic distance.

I floated in my mind from Nebraska to the mercy and graciousness of Robert and Joanne, who reached out and gave us a place to stay when we were storm refugees without a home despite no familial connection at all. And I began to see acts of love of all kinds and sizes at every point in between Nebraska and my mother's house and beyond. From inspiration across generations, to the texts and messages of friends and family checking in, to the late-night worries and prayers, to the helping hand of a stranger reaching from atop an airboat. Throughout this journey, it was always there.

Gravity could not restraint it, nor time constrain it. And water would not wash it away. Like the corona dancing at the edge of totality, and the color on the horizon, it is beyond the reach of the abyss. Cliché though it may be, love knows no bounds. There is no match for the infinite but the infinite. Despite all that Harvey had wrought, I had ample room for hope.

XIII. A New Hope

Hope comes in many forms. On that morning, it first came in the form of a friend, Kevin, waiting by his car with his work gloves already on, arriving before I had even made it to the house. He was eager to help. Hope came shortly thereafter in my Uncle Glenn, and my friend Randy, who had forgiven me for not attending his fight night party. It arrived with Dedra and the kids, with friends Tom and his son Matthew, and with friends Kathy, John, and their son Andrew. All of them there to lighten my burden. They worked tirelessly, graciously.

Their many hands made much lighter work, and with each of their steps mine grew stronger. Hope can arrive as simply as a homemade ham sandwich and a Gatorade when my muscles began to seize. Karen's lunch and the even more brought by Kathy gave our entire crew of helpers fuel throughout the day. Hope came throughout the neighborhood and beyond as volunteers began arriving to undertake a massive city-wide cleanup effort. Everyone worked tirelessly into the evening.

The next day brought more hands. My sister, Lisa, and brother-in-law, Brian, greeted Kevin and me at the front door, bright and early, as the day two crew was assembling. They had water as high as their garage in their own Bellaire area home on the other side of Houston. It was good to see them safe, and I let them in through the front door entryway, which had served as the decontamination zone between the flood and the shelter upstairs. Upon the table, remnant equipment from the successful power shutdown procedure remained, i.e., the rubber-glove-adorned baseball bat.

"I'm not even going to ask," Brian said as he glanced at the lifesaving device.

"Oh, that. Yeah, it's kind of a long story. Maybe I'll share it during the holidays," I laughed and welcomed him in.

"Maybe not," he said with a returning laugh. And then he went straight to work adding to the growing pile in our front yard of discarded furniture, clothes, carpets, our entire downstairs contents. My sister Lisa was carefully accounting for it all with her usual eye for every detail. It was all laid bare in the sun—Harvey's spoils. All along the back end of our neighborhood the trash began to pile up. It was a scene that was repeated in thousands of neighborhoods across the region over the next several weeks as the waters began to recede. Walls of trash, as tall as six-feet high, lined the streets of hundreds of thousands of homes. Where they put all of this trash, I still have no idea.

At our house, everyone worked hard. Our contractor for the upcoming recovery project was a friend with whom I had coached Little League baseball last season. He and a couple of his workers showed up and began ripping out the downstairs walls at about 4' all around, while my family and friends worked in between them. Our trash wall outside was growing ever longer and higher. Inside, the hardwood floor began to buckle as it dried under the weight of the piano, and its legs appeared misaligned under the shifting floor.

"Dad!" Grace shouted at me to come observe it. She seemed concerned. "Is the piano ruined?"

"It may be. None of us can move it out. So, it could be just another victim of Harvey," I responded frankly.

"Are you sad? You loved that piano." She was more concerned with my feelings than hers. She's always had a sensitive heart, which she cannot mask even behind her teenage bravado. She knew it was my favorite piece of furniture.

I smiled. "You know, I did enjoy hacking around on that piano."

Mostly, it reminded me of my father who could actually play the piano exceptionally well, but it was my sister, Kimberly, who inherited his musical talent. I just liked to fiddle around from time to time, much to the annoyance of my captive listening audience.

I continued, "But, you know something, that piano never once gave me a hug. It never pulled me into a boat, or gave me a hot meal and a warm, dry bed. So, it was never really worth *loving*. All of this is just stuff." I motioned around to the piano and remaining trashed furniture in the room. "You can't love stuff, because stuff can't love you back."

"That's nice, Dad. But it still stinks," she said in that *okay, don't get all pedantic again* voice she reserves for, well, when I get pedantic.

"Yeah, it stinks," I acknowledged.

And it did stink—literally as well as figuratively. The dank, musty smell haunted everything that Harvey bathed with his waters. It was both foul and potentially dangerous given the billions of mold spores growing in the dampness of the drying walls and floors, and everything in between. On the prior day, Kathy conducted a search of every hardware store in a 15-mile radius for respirators for the additional helping hands we had on our work crew. Our neighbors Jack and Laurie pitched in with additional cleaning supplies they had as well. All along our street, and on streets all around the city, friends, families, volunteers, everyone worked feverishly cleaning the mess.

Indeed, throughout Houston supplies were running scarce as the number of Harvey evacuees was far bigger than imagined. Yet, hope arrived with every blanket or bottle of water passed out by rescue workers, *guys in boats*, or one of the now thousands of helping hands who emerged from their dry homes with broom and mop at the ready. We had no riots. Harvey's minions of despair were met by even more helping hands of hope. For those first days in Houston after the storm, we had only two kinds of folks in town: storm victims and helpers.

I was reminded of a childhood hero, Fred Rogers, aka Mr. Rogers, whose calming wisdom helped me pass afternoons after school as a small boy. Once, when he was asked about handling tragedy with children, he said:

When I was a boy and I would see scary things on the news, my mother would say to me, "Look for the helpers. You will always find people who are helping."

I suppose it was actually the wisdom of his mother. I can relate. In any event, everywhere in Houston, in the midst of the devastation and tragedy, we saw those who took action to help their fellow citizens who were scared and suffering from the despair brought by Harvey's wrath. We were looking for the helpers. And the helpers were there. They were creators of hope with actions, large and small.

More than a thousand miles away, hope came in a different form. A man who can throw a baseball very hard made a decision to take a chance on a city he didn't know, to play for a team in the midst of a big slump. With just two minutes left before the final Major League Baseball trade deadline, Justin Verlander, a grizzled veteran ace from the Detroit Tigers, agreed to join the Houston Astros. To a team that had been hit hard by the storms of August and the displacement of Harvey, he brought the same kind of *roll up the sleeves and get to work attitude* that the volunteer helpers around the city had. When he took the mound, he went to work in a way that re-ignited the fire that had driven the Astros to a record-breaking spring and early summer. He pitched a month of September that matched in greatness the dominance of Randy Johnson's short stint for the Astros in 1997. He won *every* game he started, allowing only one run per nine innings he pitched. The team's confidence was rejuvenated, and September brought them a long-awaited division title. Houston "literally loved Justin Verlander."

It would not be understatement to say that the people of Houston began to look to the Astros for more than just baseball. We were emotionally vested in the team more than ever before. They became more than merely a distraction in the evenings to follow a day of full of dealing with the storm recovery. It's as if we were victims of Harvey together and were fighting together to overcome what he had wrought.

In the days and weeks that would follow the storm, sports would often serve as a refuge. My friend Darren drove all the way in from Austin to pick me up and take me out to dinner, a beer, and the opening night game for college football season. Florida State's hopes were diminished with the loss of their quarterback in the first half, but mine were raised by our fellowship around the game. I forgot about the flood for a while, his kind deed accomplishing its goal, and we enjoyed good conversation for as much of the Alabama-Florida State game as I could watch before succumbing to fatigue. I appreciated his kind deed and the reminder that sports offered an escape for a little while. But there was no team whose heart beat with ours like the Astros. The Astros were not an escape. It almost seemed as if our hopes were invested in them, if not aligned with them. I think that could be said for a goodly portion of the city.

It was certainly true for my friend and colleague, Toby, who also suffered from two feet of floodwaters washing through his house. During the long, ongoing, recovery process we buried ourselves deeper in the Astros as the tedium of the recovery efforts stirred our anxieties. With friends, Randy and Brad, we exchanged conversations about each game and provided our best unsolicited advice to one another on how the Astros could get to the World Series. We were all in it together.

September brought hope beyond the baseball diamond. Our clean-out efforts were completed with the assistance of Dedra's mother who drove in to help box all surviving items for storage upstairs. She performed with the efficiency and organization indicative of her career as a school principal. We were spending days at our house cleaning and boxing and nights at my mother's sleeping and doing laundry. It was an extraordinarily hectic time. When my mother's dryer broke down on the first night, my aunt and uncle Ann and Dennie were over with a hot meal and a new belt replacement. Help came from every direction, and always when we needed it most.

Our downstairs was gutted to the studs about half way down the walls in the first days of September. We took what we needed to my mother's house and let the bleaching process proceed. It was to be a cleansing. We adjusted to the commute back and forth from Friendswood to Pasadena, but it was grinding. Robert and Joanne exceeded their first act of graciousness by bounds, offering their own prior home as a place to stay while our house was repaired. It was such a blessing to have a place to stay much nearer the kids' schools, and we can never thank them enough for the outpouring of love that they have selflessly provided.

Alex's question would be answered. He would miss a week more of school due to closure. But that was a week *after* we actually figured out what day of the week it was. In total, I believe the kids were out of school for more than two weeks. It took several days before things settled in enough for us to shift from our stone-aged *three days after the rescue* or *the day before Mom got to town* calendaring. Dedra and I got back into our work cycles, but not into routine.

Support came from all over. From my aunt and uncle Marilyn and Bob in California to friends in Minnesota, who had some baseball dreams of their own at the time. Hope came with a boss who sat me down and told me to "take time to deal with the storm"—she only half-jokingly called it an *order*. She did this despite knowing that her workload would increase because of it. My colleagues were equally as understanding and kind. Friends, family, Grace's entire soccer team, Dedra's colleagues all brought us dinners throughout our displacement warming our bellies along with our hearts. Everywhere there were acts of kindness and love to buoy our displaced

Greg Etzel

spirits. We were so fortunate.

Others far less so. Across the city, shelters and volunteers continued to work to meet the needs of the lost and forgotten survivors still needing assistance. Houston's most famous furniture store owner and great philanthropist, Jim McIngvale (lovingly known in these parts as *Mattress Mack*), offered his own business as a shelter for the displaced during the early recovery, sacrificing large amounts of his inventory to provide a refuge for those without an alternative. Throughout September and beyond, he donated many items of furniture to victims of the storm. Other businesses, religious organizations, and civic groups banded together to furnish the hope that people affected by the storm craved. Houston's most famous adopted Texan, JJ Watt, championed the cause using his good name and time to raise millions of dollars in relief funding as people from around the nation turned their attention toward us. The city was living up to its newly minted slogan—Houston Strong.

Working at the house one afternoon toward the end of our clean-up process, I saw a man in a truck that had pulled off just to the side by our street. He was looking to move our old kitchen table that was tossed out along the street amongst the giant wall of discarded furniture and growing mounds of sheetrock and wood planks into his truck. He began to walk away as I approached, but I stopped him and offered to help him load it. I saw in his eyes the look I had when I stood beneath the man in the airboat in chest high water with my bag strapped on my back and rain pouring on me. I helped him load up the chairs that went with the table, and told him to help himself to any other pieces he could find amongst the wall. As we chatted, we could tell from our faces and hands that we had traveled down different paths. Nevertheless, they converged at a moment when we both faced each other as human beings needing other human beings. That furniture had never been more valuable to me than in that moment.

As the calendar turned to October, I stood in my gutted downstairs still anxiously awaiting what the assessment would be from our insurance company. With so many claims, so many repairs, and so much devastation throughout the region, delay became the expectation and not the exception. I was displaced and uncertain. We still faced a host of hurdles to getting back to normal. But my experience has taught me this truth—insurance companies and construction workers are not the ones responsible for recovery. True recovery comes from the kindness and love of friends and family. And that we had received in abundance.

On the first day of October, I stood alone in the empty downstairs of my house. The walls were gutted and stripped bare. Yet, I have never felt so complete.

XIV. Sometimes It's More Than Just a Game

Only one thing remained, really. And that was for the Houston Astros to finish the story. After all, our August struggles and September recovery seemed inextricably intertwined with theirs. We had been through the storm together. Their story was our story. And this was not just true for our household. As Houston communities continued to dig out from the storm and navigate the giant piles of trash lining every neighborhood street, the city became one with the Astros in a way that I had never seen before. By October, it had settled in for everyone that recovery from Harvey was going to be a *very* long process. Throughout the daily toils of cleanup and salvage efforts in September and early October, the Astros played on, marching in step with the labors of every Houstonian. By mid-October they found themselves marching past the Boston Red Sox and into the American League Championship Series for the first time in franchise history. A recovering city looked to the Astros to furnish it with a symbol. They played for us all.

The ALCS brought a chance for the Astros's first trip to the World Series since 2005, when they lost in four straight games. That 2005 trip, which they made as a National League team, was the first in the city's now 55-year history of baseball. They were now an American League team, and I will spare you my description of how that transpired. Needless to say, the Astros played in the American League now and could be the first team to represent both leagues in the World Series.

To get to the World Series, they would have to face the most storied franchise in baseball history —those damned New York Yankees—who had found themselves a brand-new star in their galaxy of talent by the name of Aaron Judge. Judge was the most feared power hitter in all of baseball, hitting 52 home runs in this, his rookie season, more than any other first-year hitter in history. He stood like a giant on the field, towering over the Houston Astros's best player, José Altuve, giving further impression to the David-Goliath nature of this Championship Series. The Astros had the better record of the two teams, but when it came to star power and media attention, Houston was no match for New York.

Obviously, like most Houstonians, we watched every game with intense interest. No one more so than Harrison, who made sure I knew what time the game was on every night. Harrison loves playing baseball. He would practice or mess around with the ball and bat at any opportunity. I was grateful he had older brothers, for as the youngest child he inherited a father with seven years less energy than I had with my first born, Zach. Harrison had kept a watchful eye on the Astros from his earliest days, accompanying his brothers, sister, and me to many a game. Few boyhood passions run deeper than a favorite sports team, regardless of the sport. And few men can attract the attention of a boy more than his favorite player. Harrison watched the

Astros, and one player in particular, with a zeal that was contagious. In him, I saw my boyhood self, cheering on my favorite Astros team in one of their historical playoff runs. Harrison exhibited an eagerness of expectation in his excitement for every game, a confidence that the Astros would win tonight no matter what.

Yet, though I could recognize his zeal, I was unable to obtain it, burdened as I was by memories of past playoff failures that weighed like anchors on my hopes. Astros history offered only experiences of anguish, of heart-rending losses, of *just not quite enough* moments, with every playoff run. It was my children, unburdened by these historic woes, who would chide me when I would let the doubt from 48 years of experiences with dashed playoff dreams cause me to give in to despair.

Such was the case in Game 4 of the ALCS in New York. The Astros were ahead of the Yankees in the series, two games to one, and Astros's starting pitcher Lance McCullers was pitching a dominant game, holding a 4-0 lead in the seventh inning. The Astros's manager, AJ Hinch, pulled McCullers when he gave up a solo home run to the behemoth Aaron Judge. When he made the move, I let out a string of expletives that would have made a sailor blush. I felt the playoff series slipping away in the moments to follow as the bullpen gave up five runs to blow a 4-1 lead and lost the game. I began to believe that this would end like every other disappointing Houston Astros playoff story. But, Harrison, whose nine years

of recent baseball experience in Little League and
beyond gave him a wisdom beyond his years,
inspired me to remember that we had another game
tomorrow.

Well, that all worked fine and dandy until the
Astros found themselves in Game 7 of the ALCS
against those mighty New York Yankees, where
there *was* no tomorrow for the loser. Harry
suggested that we go out to eat at a local pizza
place that we had tried out during Game 2 of the
same ALCS—a game that we won. This imbued a
sort of charm on the establishment, and as Harry
knows from batting against pitchers almost twice his
size, baseball players will do anything they think will
bring good luck on the baseball diamond. We all
accepted his suggestion and watched the game as a
lesser known of the Astros pitching staff took the
mound—Charlie Morton. "Uncle Charlie" my friends
and I called him, spelling Charlie in our texts with a
"K" after strikeouts. He had a pretty good stint in
Pittsburgh for a number of years, and had been a
strong contributor for the Astros all season, but he
didn't have the resume of a star pitcher one would
expect in the final game of a league championship
series. A real question hovered around him as to
whether he would be able to shoulder the moment.
Something about his performance in Game 3 of this
same series, where he gave up seven earned runs
and lost may have had something to do with that
question.

But he was the necessary alternative

because the other options were exhausted. The Astros's fate, like the fate of the city itself during the storm, was in the hands of the *everyman.* Charlie Morton stepped on the mound that night and pitched with the spirit and vigor of a player lifted by the need of his city. He threw five shutout innings against the second most deadly batting order in baseball, striking out five batters. In the sixth inning, he handed the ball over to Lance McCullers, and then walked off the field to the roars of a sold-out crowd who recognized in him the spirit of the men and women who stepped up to rescue or assist their neighbors merely a month ago. We joined everyone in the restaurant cheering as we recognized it ourselves.

Lance McCullers came in and finished the game. He was utterly dominant again, striking out six batters in four innings, and Hinch never once thought about replacing him. His steely-eyed glare and golden arm kept the Yankees at bay to clinch the victory. The spirit of Houston was on that mound that evening, and the Houston Astros were in the World Series!

"It looks like we'll be eating here a lot next week," Harrison said as we traded high fives all around.

I laughed at the time. But we *did* come back to that restaurant several more times during the World Series.

In the World Series, the Astros faced the Los Angeles Dodgers, who had star power and a record-breaking season of their own. Indeed, their pitching had been as legendarily good as our hitting. Though both teams won more than 100 games, the Dodgers had the better record during the season and earned home field advantage for the series. It promised to be one of the great matchups in World Series history. It would not disappoint.

The buzz throughout the city for the World Series was like nothing before, everywhere Houstonians raised banners and signs for support. With the walls of trash slowly being removed and shelters continuing to house the displaced, Houstonians craved the sense of finality that the end of the Astros's season offered even as we continued to recover. We *needed* to believe in a happy ending.

We did not go to the pizza place for Game 1, opting to dine at home instead. It was the wrong decision. The Dodger's perennial Cy Young Award winner, Clayton Kershaw, proved too dominant for Houston hitters on the hottest day for a World Series game in history. With temperatures at 100 degrees Fahrenheit at game time, Astros batters melted before Kershaw's ruthlessly efficient pitching performance. The Astros's all-star lead-off hitter, George Springer, had a particularly difficult game, going 0-4 with four strikeouts. Indeed, that is pretty much the worst game a batter can have, period. He had struggled during the Yankees series also, and all of the buzz on local sports radio and amongst friends at the water cooler the next morning was that it was time to move him down in the lineup or sit him out for a game or two. The Astros were down only one game in the World Series and the minions of doubt were creeping in like the slithery serpents on Harvey's flood tide.

But the Astros's manager kept Springer there, right at the top, telling reporters before Game 2 that he believed in what he knows his players *can* do, not what they *had* done. In other words, he had hope. Confidence that tomorrow will fulfill the promise left unmet today, that his players' talent would be enough if he just *believed* in them. Just the sort of thing that an old Astros fan and displaced Harvey survivor needed to hear. Yesterday does *not* define tomorrow. The struggles of past seasons, the heartbreaking playoff losses, the piles of sheetrock, wood planks, and warped cabinetry in the yard, the sleeping on a mattress on the floor with plastic tubs for drawers, these did not represent our fate for the future. With his act, AJ Hinch reminded us all—"It will be fine, Houston; you just have to believe in yourself."

That faith was rewarded. George Springer had *three* hits in Game 2, including the game winning home run in the eleventh inning. It was the first World Series win in the Astros's history, and they won it in dramatic fashion. Justin Verlander pitched a very solid game for Houston, but made two mistakes —both home runs that found the Astros down 3-2 in the ninth inning. Kenley Jansen, Major League Baseball's best closer, had not given up a lead in over a year when he came in to shut down the

Dodgers win that night. But Marwin Gonzalez became the first hero of a historic night with a clutch game-tying home run in the top of the ninth inning. Springer would be the last hero in a cast of superlative late-inning performances that would string together three of the most memorable innings in the history of World Series baseball. When he won it finally with a deciding eleventh-inning home run, Springer delivered on the promise of his manager. The game lasted four hours and 19 minutes, and when it was over, I celebrated with my children as if I were one of them again. We had experienced the most incredible post-season game that any Houston fan ever witnessed.

Yet, it was only the beginning. The Astros would come back home to play three games over the weekend in front of an emotional crowd, with stories of Harvey survival being shared throughout the build up to the game broadcasts. It was as clear to a national audience as it was to every Houstonian, that the Astros were engaged in more than a World Series. We watched every inning, many from our same pizza place, as the Astros traded the next two games with the Dodgers, and found themselves locked in a 2-2 series tie with a pivotal Game 5 coming on a Sunday night in Houston.

Now, when they compile the list of the ten greatest World Series games of all time, Game 5 of the 2017 World Series should be on it twice. The game featured the same starters as Game 1, Dallas Keuchel for the Astros, and the dominant Clayton

Kershaw for the Dodgers. An Astros victory meant
they would take the lead in the series with our ace,
Justin Verlander, on the mound in Game 6, when the
series shifted back to Los Angeles. To say it was a
critical game is an understatement. The crowd was
absolutely electric before the game, their energy
buzzing through our TV screens and connecting us
in time. The city watched the biggest game in its
history, now longing for fulfilment more than
distraction.

The excitement was very short-lived. Like a
band of Harvey's thunderous rains, the Dodgers
hammered the Astros for three runs in the top of the
first inning. And like Harvey's rains, those runs
brought the minions of doubt and despair. The
Dodgers added another run in the fourth, making it
4-0, while Kershaw kept the Astros scoreless
through the first three and a half innings.

"Well, that's going to do it, dammit! We let
this one get away!" I grumbled aloud as the Dodgers
fourth run crossed the plate.

"Come on, Dad. It's the fourth inning. Stop
being so negative," Harrison called me out again.

"I'm being realistic, okay. There's a
difference. Kershaw gives up four runs in a game
like never, ok. Dude has an ERA under two. And
even if he gets tired, they'll just go to their best in the
Majors bullpen." I was obviously still adjusting to this
hope thing, particularly in the context of Houston
sports.

"They came back the other night, didn't they?

You gotta believe," Harrison lectured with an urgency in his voice.

"Yeah, yeah. Hey, I'm still rooting. I'm just managing my expectations." In other words, I had doubt.

Perhaps many of us did throughout Houston. And it is something that no box score can convey. We had been battered by storms, many of us still cleaning up. We, too, faced difficult odds to overcome before we could reestablish normality in our lives. It was easy to see the four-run lead as the rising waters lapping at our door, destined to take us and leave us empty. But what good is hope if it cannot deliver us at times against long odds?

In the fourth inning, the Houston Astros unloaded against the Dodgers's titan, Kershaw. It was as if the Astros hitters forgot who they were facing and what their odds were. They simply went out and hit the ball with the joy of a child playing a game. When Yuri Guireill, the Astros's first baseman, hit the three-run shot to tie the game at 4-4, an entire city of fans exceeded their prior best vertical leap. When Kershaw finally ended the fourth inning, the Astros and the city were charged with a renewed energy.

"It's a brand-new ball game, baby!" I shouted, exchanging high fives with everyone in the living room, and absorbing the *I told you so* glance from Harrison.

Yet, no sooner than it took to resettle in our seats and grab our drinks, the Astros walked two batters and then gave up a three-run home run to the Dodger's Cody Bellinger. We were right back where we started. It was *exactly* like the storm. Doubt and despair would not relent. Down by three again with Kershaw still pitching and the Dodger bullpen ready to pick up the slack. I sank in my seat, almost regretting the elation I had just felt, as if it were somehow less meaningful now. Alex saw the forlorn look on my face and prompted me to acknowledge that the game was not over—far from it.

Sometimes hope comes in unexpected shapes. If you were to line up all of the players in the major leagues and pick a team based solely on their outward appearance, José Altuve might be the last player picked. In every nationally broadcast game, there is always a story about his diminutive 5' 5" build in comparison to the much larger players around him. Indeed, looking at him, you'd think he has no place being in the Major Leagues. But, just ask Yoda about judging people by their size.

José Altuve not only made it to Major League Baseball, he became its most valuable player. He did it because he didn't care about the odds. He did it because he didn't care about the insults and the taunts growing up in the game, and the questions from every reporter about his height. He did it because he loved baseball. He did it because he worked on his game with the attention of a good farmer to his fields, grinding through every day to improve. He did it because he can see pitches better than any other batter. But most of all, he became the game's greatest player because he *believed* in himself. Altuve out-hit, out-hustled, and out-matched any doubt that ever presented itself to him. Like the good farmer who toils through every step of the planting process with faith that the rains will come, Altuve played the game believing he would succeed.

This is the stuff that can inspire a scrawny 14-year old, about a year or so behind the growth curve of every pitcher and batter he faces, to continue playing baseball with his own new team. There was no such thing as being too small to play, and Harrison worked his way up from the bottom of the order to the middle with every hit or hustle play he made during his season. Harrison knew that Altuve had to get the coach's attention on the field, not on paper—with effort and hustle. And that no substitute exists in baseball for believing in yourself.

Like the rest of the city, although perhaps with a bit more personal feelings invested, Harrison sat glued to the TV as José Altuve stepped up to the plate in the bottom of the fifth inning with two outs and two runners on base, with the Astros trailing by three runs. In a single stroke of the bat, José Altuve returned our living room and the entire city to euphoria with a three-run bomb. There was an even brighter glow on Harrison's face as he danced around the living room, and on every kid's face that seems outsized at times. Altuve was an MVP beyond the game.

His home run had once again tied the game,

179

now at 7-7, but the emotional roller coaster ride was not over. The Dodgers would once again take the lead in the seventh inning, 8-7, only to be bested by the Astros, who scored four runs in the bottom of the seventh to go ahead for the first time 11-8. But, the Dodgers refused to go away, chipping away in the eighth inning to make the game closer at 11-9. Those in the crowd (and on their sofas watching the game with their children) who were made nervous by the Dodger's run in the eighth, were revived by Brian McCann's homer for the Astros in the bottom of the eighth inning. It was 12-9 Astros, a three-run lead with only one half of an inning to go. People were beginning to dance in the aisles of the stadium.

If you could only run out the clock in baseball. But you can't. You have to get outs. The Astros's Chris Devenski, or *Devo,* as the fans called him, took the mound in the top of the ninth with a three-run lead and the weight of the dreams of 6.5 million Houstonians on his shoulders. That can be an awful lot. Despite being one of the Astros's most reliable relievers during the season, he was tired and could not keep the command of his pitches that he once had. Like the reservoirs around town that could not handle the load of Harvey's rains, the Dodgers' relentless bats broke through the best levy Devo could muster, and the Dodgers tied the game with three runs. It was the third lead change of three or more runs in a single game. No World Series game in the 113-year history of the series had ever featured as many dramatic large-lead changes.

Against the Storm

The dancing had stopped. Shoulders that were bouncing slumped, and eyes looked down. Every emotional swing throughout the game was magnified by the city's longing for relief. The fresh memories of our struggles with Harvey came unbridled back to the surface of our minds with each heave and ho of the game. Back and forth, back and forth, the mighty teams had fought through the night and literally into the next day. Every pitcher in the bullpen, every strategy at hand, every effort was made by both teams to overcome their equally matched foe. With them, the fans ebbed and flowed, torn apart by emotional extremes, pacing, jumping, or slouching and grumbling. Finally, after five hours and 17 minutes, a young new star from Louisiana named Alex Bregman delivered a hit in the bottom of the tenth inning that gave Houston fans the final cheer of elation, and it served as a fitting tribute to the *Cajun Navy* who had come through when Houston needed it during the storm. It was one of the longest games in World Series history. When it was finally over, there was little left but exhaustion, cramping, and adrenaline-fueled joy. And I'm sure the players experienced some of that, too.

The next day was a day off so that the teams could travel back to Los Angeles for the finale. The fans needed a rest as much as the players after Game 5. Sportswriters all around quickly acknowledged it as one of, if not the, greatest World Series game of all time. And yet, that only took into consideration what was happening on the field. In the stands, and in the living rooms throughout

Houston, there was a lot more going on than a game. We relived the storm during Game 5, wave after wave of emotion pounding us like Harvey's rains and our responses to them. We needed that game to end with a win because that's how we needed to remember the storm—it was a battle, but we had emerged in victory. Say what you will, I believe it was the most important World Series game to a city in the history of baseball.

But it was only the *third* win, one more was still necessary for a championship. It was, however, the prevailing notion that Houston would be the heavy favorites to win Game 6 with Justin Verlander on the mound for us. With this confidence, we conducted our affairs over the course of the next two days waiting to celebrate the presumptive World Series title on Halloween. Toby and I fought hard to contain our glee at work over those days, not wanting to openly convey that positive outcome in which we had convinced ourselves internally to believe. Obviously, we had to play the game, and you can never take them for granted, yada, yada, yada. But, we felt the title was in our hands on the last day of October.

As if synchronized across Houston, our porch light went off at 7:08 PM that evening, discouraging potential trick-or-treaters from interrupting our soon-to-be celebration. We didn't want to go out to the pizza place, however, because we thought we might face too much Halloween traffic. Harrison would not let me forget that decision.

Against the Storm

An early home run by George Springer and dominant first five innings by Verlander had the Astros looking good. But Verlander gave up two runs in the sixth inning and that was all the Dodgers would need to support their commanding pitching performance. It was a punch-to-the gut loss, and the World Series was tied 3-3 with the Dodgers having home field advantage for the decisive seventh game. The Champagne went back on ice, and it may have moved locker rooms.

At work the next day, I'd never seen Toby look so despondent. Generally, I depend on Toby to cheer me up, as he is the most positive person I know. I found myself in his customary shoes.

"You know what, it's ok. This can't go down as the greatest World Series of all time if it doesn't go to a Game 7," I tried to prop him up.

"We had our chance last night. That was the night," he replied still stuck deeply in yesterday's soul-crushing defeat.

"But if we had won last night, who will remember the greatness of this series? It *has* to go seven. That's just how the story *has* to end." I tried to put a spin on it as if to suggest that even in defeat, playing to Game 7 secures the legendary status of the series and epic nature of Game 5. I thought of Achilles and the choice of living forever in obscurity or dying young with immortal fame. Achilles took the latter because he knew his name would live long past his flesh. "Win or lose, this series will always be remembered as the greatest," I urged in positivity.

"Are you trying to sell me on a *Rocky*-type victory?" He was of course referencing the famous Sylvester Stalone movie in which Rocky loses a split decision, but is the winner in everyone's heart because he came from long odds to go toe-to-toe with the champ.

"Look, you never know. You just gotta believe," I found myself channeling my children again, their youthful spirit overcoming my aged-cynicism. Watching the series with them *had* eroded my pessimism and gave me the strength to pass on their hope to others.

And with the conversation, hope began to grow in me. We may be short on pitching, and the Dodgers may have Kershaw to use for several innings in the later part of the game, but anything goes in a Game 7 and anything can happen. It occurred to me that, if in Game 5 we re-lived the storm and, by virtue of the victory, the initial clean up, then in Game 6 we relived the disappointing calls from insurance companies telling us that "we won't be able to get that estimate until sometime in November" or from one inspector or another giving us news of lengthy delays. Game 6 was the reality that comes after the initial euphoria of the storm's passing. Game 6 reminded us that not everything goes as we expect it to go.

When I arrived home from work that evening, I was greeted at the door by Harrison.

"Dad, I don't care what you say, we are *going* to the pizza place tonight," he said it with the gravest of necessities in his tone.

"You had me at, *Dad,* Harrison. You had me at *Dad.*" We had entirely too much at stake for any other option. My hopes were lifting despite the odds, buoyed by both my growing tendency to see the World Series as an extension of our own flood experience, and by the example that Harrison and the kids had provided throughout the earlier games. With the outpouring of love and support that we had received after the storm and the perspective it had given me, I was more confident in a positive recovery. And my children had already convinced me that my prior 48-years of baseball fan experience had no bearing on the game that was being played that night. Somehow, before the game even started, I knew we would be all right. That being said, I was certainly not willing to risk my new-found hope by *not* going to the pizza place.

In the city, Minute Maid Ballpark was filled to capacity, despite having no players on the field. Thousands of fans had piled in to watch the Astros together on the giant stadium screen. Some watched from restaurants and bars. Some watched from a TV plugged into a generator in a room with gutted out walls. But *everybody* watched.

We all wanted to know how this storybook ends.

XV. Forward to the Horizon

In this, the greatest World Series of all time, most sportswriters would tell you that Game 7 was the least dramatic of the series. But that's because they only consider the box score. The Astros came into the game with serious questions as to how they would find the pitching to stop the Dodgers. Everyone was exhausted. Hell, we were all exhausted. Our family, our city, all strained to the emotional limit, looking for baseball to rescue us from the storm.

Lance McCullers, the number three starter, would start, but he could only get through two innings. However, in those two innings the Astros bats came alive, including a home run from the soon-to-be World Series MVP, George Springer, and they staked the Astros to a big five-run lead. Yes, it was that same George Springer whose manager had faith in him when few others did. Yes, it was the player with *the* most embarrassing Game 1 in World Series history, who would go on to become its MVP. Now, you tell me how that happens without hope?

Clinging to the five-run lead in the bottom of the fifth inning, and with a bullpen that was shaky at best, AJ Hinch turned once again to Charlie Morton —*Uncle Charlie.* Of course, that is how it would *have* to end. The unsung hero would need to rise to save the day. Like the thousands upon thousands of volunteers who raked out the muck and the mire from flooded homes of friends and strangers, like the *guys with boats,* like the neighbors and friends reaching out, this series had to be won for Houston by the everyman. The stars did their part, to be sure, but in the end, this was about the guy who represented a city without the glitz and glamour of Los Angeles or New York; a city where hope resides in the character of the guy next door. This is what was meant to be from the very beginning. This wasn't just the World Series; this was Houston's recovery story.

Charlie Morton took the mound in the fifth inning, and he never left the game. He gave up a single run, but otherwise rolled up his sleeves and worked through the Dodgers like a skilled craftsman. When the final out was recorded by none other than José Altuve with a giant grin on his face—one that matched the boyish one across Harrison's at the exact same moment—it was history. Charlie Morton won Game 7, and we danced in the restaurant and embraced each other with a spirited exuberance. The city exploded in celebration. Houston had its first World Series championship, and one that meant more than any of the players would ever know.

If you would have asked every sports analyst in the country before the 2017 season who would be the winning pitcher for Game 7 of the American League Championship Series *and* for Game 7 of the World Series exactly zero would have picked Charlie Morton. That's because the sports experts rely on historical performance data, and cannot accurately account for chance—or destiny.

Now, I suppose there are some that will say that all of this was just chance. That it was a random accident in the unfolding of space and time that I happened to make a journey to gaze into the totality of the first solar eclipse in the United States in 100 years, returned to my home town to face a *thousand-year storm* in the Astros season with just the right cast of characters, with a World Series that unfolded with dramatic emotional swings and epic-length games mimicking the very storm itself. That everything from my trip to Nebraska to the last out of the World Series was just a series of unconnected coincidences seeming to align to create a narrative. I guess that case could be made.

But, if you ask me, I think it's something more. In any event, I knew it was not *chance* that gave me the faith to keep cheering when times were tough. I knew it was not *chance* that reached out to pull me up from the floodwaters, or provided me a nice bed and a warm meal, or that showed up ready to lend a hand when I needed help. And I don't think it was *chance* that my story started in Nebraska, moved through sun and storm and space, and ended up in the arms of family. It was something much better than chance. It was hope. And if it was all just chance, well, then I'm grateful that hope does not take account of the odds.

We took the day off on Friday after the game to drive into downtown for the team victory parade. It was the most crowded I've ever witnessed downtown Houston. Nearly a million people with feelings that likely matched our own jammed together in the streets in celebration and followed the parade to its end at City Hall. In the throngs of orange-clad Houstonians celebrating in those streets were storm refugees and heroes alike, sharing a moment of unity in the feeling of redemption. The Astros had delivered the ending we so desperately wanted.

With *Queen* appropriately cued on the City Hall loudspeakers, we sang with a voice a million strong. We had emerged from the storm, from the struggle, and we would be stronger by it. It was a special moment, and we all leaned closer as starting pitcher Dallas Keuchel, one of the team leaders took the microphone on the stage. He spoke out to the crowd,

"We weren't playing for you guys. We were all playing together. We won this World Series together."

We did. It seemed our fates were intertwined from the very beginning. The city celebrated as much *with* them as *for* them. It was more than just a series, more than just a game.

I looked down at my children as we celebrated with the city and saw in their faces a promise fulfilled. I felt it too, but well beyond the baseball diamond. Later that day, we learned that by official proclamation of the Governor of the State of Texas, November 3, 2017, was designated as *Houston Astros Day* in honor of the first World Series

Champions in Texas history. As it turns out, that day just happens to be Harrison's (and Grace's) birthday, which, by the way, is shared (exactly 80 years earlier) by their still-living great grandmother and her (also) twin brother who grew up in, you guessed it, Nebraska, where this story began. Now, how about that for *chance* tying this whole thing up with a nice little bow?

Alas, life is never *that* perfect. The truth is that the recovery process doesn't end with the baseball season. The road is long and sometimes hard. Displacement, repair, recovery, it all lingers on longer than anyone expects or likes. But my Harvey story ends with a World Series Championship and a city, battered by the heavy hand of nature, united a million strong in song—*We Are the Champions*.

For me, the story of Hurricane Harvey will always end on November 3, 2017. Whatever story comes next, well, that remains to be seen.

The world spins on, moving on its naturally commanded course. To be sure, the storm left its mark on me, on the city. Yet the storm will not define us. Whatever havoc Harvey wrought, he revealed the light of human spirit that beacons even in the darkest hours. A city whose neighbors take action to help neighbors survive and recover is a city of hope. It will always thrive and prosper. New opportunities lie on the horizon, and Harvey is but preface to what stories they will bring.

I share my account to bear witness to the violence of a storm and the forces of nature that we cannot control, and as a reminder of the everyday acts of kindness and love between us that lie beyond nature's reach and bind us together outside its limits of time and space. Perhaps some things in life are left to chance, but love is not one of them. It is an active choice. It is the light that shines at the edge of darkness and provides hope against the infinite abyss.

There are 6.5 million stories about Hurricane Harvey. That is mine. And if my children, or theirs, should come seeking any lesson from it, I would leave them this:

There will be storms. Do not get lost in the darkness of their skies. Look to the horizon. Create hope.

Acknowledgement:

My story is but a testament of thanks to my family, friends, colleagues, new and old, from places near and far, and from generations removed, whose many acts of love serve as my Aegis against the abyss. May my words shine as brightly as their deeds as a token of my eternal gratitude. It is a testimony of appreciation to every man, woman, and child who did so much as hand out a bottle of water to a thirsty storm victim, whose acts of kindness large and small provided the promise of a better tomorrow to me, and to an entire city. And, yes, it is a tribute to a baseball team that took on the emotional burden of a city for more than just a game and redeemed their long-awaited hopes.

www.ingramcontent.com/pod-product-compliance
Lightning Source LLC
Chambersburg PA
CBHW060849280326
41934CB00007B/978